A Hole In My Heart the 'SIZE OF MY FATHER'

Written by

Cognitive Behavioral Therapist,

Patric Paul Garrett

ClearEdge Press Publishing

PO Box 1262
12400 Ventura Blvd
Studio City, CA 91604

A Hole In My Heart The Size Of My Father

Exploring a wealth of information our childhood has brought us, through relationships with our fathers.

Note To Readers

This book is to help people take positive steps toward gaining awareness of their true feelings. It's not a substitute for therapy or a quick fix to mental health care. If you are experiencing any thoughts of suicide, depression, anxiety or anger please explore the guidance of mental health professionals.

To insure no further heartbreak, all my case studies, testimonies, interviews and personal conversations detailed here, the names have been changed and the identifying details have been adjusted to protect the privacy of the individuals involved. I use real life examples of father present or father absent homes to demonstrate the affects those homes has had on adult decisions.

Table of Contents

Introduction

May our sons be as strong plants grown up in their youth and that our daughters be as beautiful cornerstones of a King's palace." - Psalms 144:12

Can the child be the blame for a fatherless home? Absolutely not! Fatherless children are innocent and are only trying to fill the void left by their absent fathers. That open wound that can only be healed with an understanding of his/her father's absence. Let's try to understand why it's important for a person to understand what it does to them not to have a father around. They may not even recognize it's a problem until they're in a relationship or even have kids of their own. It may be triggered when they see someone else deal with their fathers or watch a movie, read a book with subjects centered around father-child interactions. It's okay to have those feelings, but my book speaks to what to do with those feelings of abandonment and how you can compartmentalize those feelings instead of "acting out" because of them. Those "acting out" moments will add up and begin to shape who you are and who you'll become as an adult.

I remember on one gorgeous Saturday afternoon in Southern California, my mother dragging my younger brother and I to a political rally. As a rambunctious little boy, my idea of a Saturday afternoon did not consist of me jostling for position in a crowd of adults to hear someone give a speech. So, I asked her, "Who is this person, and what makes them so important?" She tells me. "It's not always who's speaking, but who's listening." It was one of my mother's many mantras that I've adopted and use in my work with children and young adults. Over my 30 years of speaking to thousands of youth and young adults, I've been intensely listening to them and what made them who they were and who they'll later come to be. I've counseled a rainbow of races with varying economic and social statuses. However, all my findings led me to the effects of the missing father.

The most honest thing I could do was to write this book with facts and experiences that readers can relate to. I intend to provide a working tool to better understand people who had or have abusive fathers, absent fathers, or no father at all, but more importantly, to help them to understand themselves better. My exploration starts with an overview of philosophical and scientific paradigms related to the latest research about the nature of fatherless children and the effects it carries into their adulthood. Growing up without a father leaves a person feeling empty inside or what I refer to as a hole in their heart. That hole is where vital instructions, memories, and experiences are lost forever. Those who are fatherless create emotions based off of those stolen or what they would call robbed of experiences. Past experiences which are our now emotions are so complex, it defines us and shows up in nearly everything dealing in our present. Our wants, our needs, our beliefs, and our preferences are all sums of our history. Now, it's determined that early childhood experiences are intricately imbedded into our being, and we can attribute that to how we treat future relationships. When learning how to ride a bike, you fall, you crash, you scrape your knees. Having a father around to comfort you and encourage you to get back up and try it again has an incomparable value. The pain in the knee will only last a moment, but the pain of feeling abandoned by a father will last a lifetime. There are things, particularly in your adult life, that happens so dramatically that you know you'll never be the same again. Maybe better, maybe worse -- but never the same. The presence of a father cannot be replaced. If you want to understand who you are and why you do what you do, you'll have to go back and find altering moments that changed the trajectory of your life. You have to understand the past to shape your future, but you cannot remain locked in those past experiences that damage your emotions and create unhealthy and unproductive signatures to your life. Though most people deal with signatures in silence, they struggle to understand how those silent emotions contribute heavily to their life decisions. It affects the jobs they take, the lovers they choose, even the schools they attend for the careers they want. TD Jakes said it best in his religious sermon entitled HEMOTIONS.*"For a man, a father is a guide to a boy. He announces to a boy what he will become. He explains to him how to chart your course through the chaos of masculinity to arrive at the destination that you have in view. And without a father there and no matter how great and wonderful a mother is, it is a liability to a son not to have a father, because there are some things that Momma cannot teach you. For a woman, a father is not a mother; this is true. But that is exactly why women need them. A father plays a critical role from childhood to young adult. He gives daughters a secure base from which a woman learns to explore the world, establish self-esteem, create independence, and to better handle everyday stressors.".* More than 23 million children live in fatherless homes. That's 23 million future parents that may or may not understand the importance of having a father in the home, possibly because they didn't have one growing up themselves. Some may feel that they are just fine without a father and believe that not having one around had no effect on them and their adult lives. Therefore, they feel comfortable raising their children without a father in the home and believe that their kids will be just fine. Then others will feel the total opposite, and they understand the hardships of the absentee father and vow to keep him in their children's lives by any means necessary.

Often, this can be life-threatening because a mother will stay in an unhealthy relationship with a toxic partner, considering the absent father from their childhood. This can potentially be detrimental to a child and their upbringing. In both examples, the common denominator is the father and the influence he will have in the long term. The immediate effects on many fatherless children and young adults are physical, but the emotional scars last longer. Depression, anxiety, fear, and loneliness is an everyday occurrence that shadows them throughout their lives. By the numbers, it's more epidemic culturally in some groups than others. In 2012, the Census Bureau reported that 57% of African Americans, 31% Hispanic, and 20% of White children were living absent of their biological fathers. This issue has had a tremendous impact on the social fabric of our society for far too long, and it's something that demanded our attention. As of 2020, the Census Bureau reports a drop in the number of children to father-absent homes by 2.5%, which is positive, but within the last five-year period, that percentage has fluctuated by less than 1%. It's dysfunctional, problematic, and long-lasting with ramifications that not only affect our children but hinder society all as a whole. I have constructed a list of different scenarios, behavioral facts, interviews, and personal experiences to demonstrate the importance of having a father's support while growing up. I plan to describe my findings from children in their adolescent, young adult, and adult stages to present a comprehensive analysis and interpretation of their past and current state.

My hypothesis will show that abandoned individuals see things from a more challenging perspective than that of a child growing up with both parents in the home. It changes a person's psyche, and it continues to change them until they get some type of resolve. We're walking among a society of broken hearts, and what's a body without the functionality of the heart? It's dead or dying! The heart is the center of the total personality, especially with reference to intuition, feeling, and emotion. It's the innermost part of everything inside us. So, one can conclude that the breaking of a heart and living with a broken heart can derail a person's development at an early age or kill a person in their elderly ages. Have you ever heard of older couples dying within months of each other because of a lonely heart? It happens. When the heart hurts, the rest of the body suffers. The heart is the essential part of a person, and when it's empty, that person is lost and wondrous. A broken heart can be mended, heartache can be soothed, but a hole in your heart can only be filled with what created it. That one missing piece that's exclusively designed to fit its shape and for the fatherless, it's the father. He plays a critical role from childhood to adulthood, but like a hole, it can be filled by other things, like hope, love, or courage. In addition, it can also be occupied by hate, distrust, resentment, isolation, and anger, which is worse because anger can poison a broken heart and contaminate the whole body.

For this reason, working as a counselor, I received plenty of firsthand accounts of children, young adults, and the homeless, all dealing with fatherlessness. Good people who experienced feelings that they were unwanted and unworthy of love. They carried that pain well into their adulthood and, as a result, experienced some unfortunate and unnecessary circumstances. Feelings of resentment and thoughts of being cheated of significant parts in their lives were glaringly perpetual. I'm not concluding that fatherlessness is the sole reason people are struggling emotionally, but I am concluding that it is the origin of an emotional and behavioral domino effect in their lives. People not knowing or being abandoned by their biological father is the most significant family problem facing America today. It's an overwhelming amount of families affected by this, and the numbers aren't decreasing fast enough. I challenge you to research your friends, co-workers, relatives, even strangers and find out how many of them grew up without a father. Whether he was emotionally or physically absent, the numbers will astonish you. If you know of someone or you were raised without a father in the home, and you're curious about what effects that may have played in your decision making, you'll find value in my book. It could have subconsciously affected your choice of career, marital partner, and even your religion. It doesn't matter how sophisticated, successful, or confident and wise a person may seem, at one time or another, the wound underneath it will all surface. The purpose of me writing this book is to give a voice to the voiceless and to ultimately seek freedom for those who've had a blockade of emotional awareness to not having a father around.

In that, there will be a clear understanding of one's self and answers to those who never knew how much an absent father dictates their lives today. I put thought to paper and turned paper into pages, and within those compiled pages, I found value. Value, I wanted to share with virtually a fatherless generation with unanswered questions. "Why am I like this?" and "How can I change?". After reading and comprehending the "Why's" and "How's," there was a discovery of self and self-awareness that gave them a sense of purpose. A Hole In My Heart The Size Of My Father can help you or someone you know to identify with the relationships they've had or the lessons they've learned, whether it's self-control, anger, anxiety, a sense of character, integrity, or accountability. Use these chapters as a guide to better yourself or help better understand those around you, such as a friend, a lover, a son, a daughter, or even your parents. I encourage you to read on, and I guarantee that you'll find someone that fits a mold in these pages. The chapters ahead take you through an introspective look at fatherless children and speak to them in a language that they can understand as adults today.

I'm the middle boy of a five children household: three boys and two younger sisters. I have a mother and a father, and we are a family. I was loved, and I'd never trade my life for any other. With that said, I intend to tell my story of how not knowing my biological father has affected every aspect of my life. In particular, decision making. Along the way, I will describe other stories from friends, counselors, classmates, girlfriends, team-mates, and strangers. I will share expert diagnosis for the problems and also statistics that back those issues. A key question I'd answer and unearthed for the fatherless child, teenager, and adult. What happened? That one question engulfs multiple meanings and has multiple answers. Once understood, it'll shed light on the relationships you form and why. You will get to know self beyond the surface while digging deeper into the make-up of you, which encompasses who, what and why you react versus respond to situations. Ultimately, you are what you are and why you feel the way you feel. The relationships you form and why. Are you ready?

On Your Mark, Get Set, Adult!

Adulthood can be thrown upon some as young as eleven years old. In some households, their responsibilities could range from caring for their adult parents to ensuring their siblings are being fed and clothed. Children with parents that are incapable of making sound decisions force their children to grow up quickly. That doesn't necessarily make those children adults, but it adds to the stressors to an already stressful journey of being a child. For the children that were catapulted into adulthood through abandonment, drug-laden parents, lack of supervision by working parents, or what's referred to as the latch-key kid, all understand that abrupt responsibilities overshadow the innocence of their childhood. Many unaware children are in a hurry to grow up and be adults, not realizing that being an adult can be quite lonely at times. That transition from being a carefree kid to a responsible deadline meeting adult can be a bit overwhelming. The first decisions we make as adults can be life-changing and wonderful or detrimental and disastrous. Thank God for our parents! These are the people that prepare their children for self-sufficiently and enable them to master a key developmental task that will carry them well into their adulthood. A mother and a father make up the word parents, and together they can support each other to give a balance to the rearing of their children. Child psychologist tells us that children have a better chance of succeeding when both parents are a part of their lives. Unfortunately, that's not always the case. What about the children that aren't raised in a two-parent household? What becomes of them? Today there's only nine-tenths of a success rate from single-parent households compared to children that come from two-parent households. When parents aren't in the lives of their children to exercise their brains and monitor their emotions, the child will be ill-prepared for the big world ahead.

Having loving parents raising children together should be the absolute norm, a definite given. In a perfect world, that would be the ideal thought pattern, but we all know this world isn't perfect, and all situations aren't ideal. When it comes to a child becoming an adult, there are many things they would have to know and be privy to. Things that could make them or break them, psychologically. The Bible states it best in Corinthians 13:11 *"When I was a child I thought as a child, but when I became a man, I put all those childish things away."*. In other words, who determines when a person becomes an adult? The rites of passage, a Bar Mitzvah? The first warrior hunt? Sex? It's not what one does, it's how one thinks, and for a child that didn't have a father around, they lack some tools and is hindered by emotional pain whether they recognize it or not. So, thinking like a child comes with what they see, hear, and feel; it can and will mold them into the potential adults they will soon become.

How do we know when we become an adult? Is it the first time we get a paying job? The first time we drink alcohol? Or when we first stand up against our parents? How about when the law recognizes us at the legal age? Each person has their own threshold of pain, emotions, and decision making before they can consider themselves an adult. I ask when do society believes you to be an adult, that's something entirely different. For the most part, it comes in the form of an assumption. Sadly, in many instances, society weighs your adulthood against the choices you've made, such as the severity of a crime committed. A perfect example is a 16-year-old Cyntoia Brown, who was forced into prostitution at an early age and was sentenced to life in prison for shooting to death an abuser out of self-defense. Without a father in her life, it allowed grimy predatory adults to manipulate her and take advantage of her youth, which led her to a jail cell in Tennessee. The court had no problem charging her as an adult, regardless of her age. She wasn't old enough to buy a lottery ticket or a pack of cigarettes, but she can do life in prison. What? Eventually, the case got overturned, and she ended up serving 10 years. Society judged her on the choices she made before the shooting and had no sympathy for her. Or how about a young athlete signing a multimillion-dollar sports contract out of high school? In some states and certain countries, society recognizes kids as adults, at the age of 16-18. Like LeBron James, the "Man Child," signing right out of high school at the age of 18. Because of what he could do among other adults, society saw him as an adult, and any "decision" he made moving forward would be questioned and scrutinized from adults. Ridiculous, he couldn't even buy alcohol or get into a night club at that age, but he can make adult decisions that will affect the rest of his life? The bottom line is, a young person doing adult activities doesn't make them an adult. Overall, it's their thinking and the ability to control it, managing their emotions, and recognizing those emotions in different climates. Sex, driving, drinking, or even having children of their own doesn't qualify a young person as an adult. People mature differently, and no one really knows you like you do. Others can assume or create some type of diagnosis about you, drawn from where you come from or what background you have, but only you know the true you. Or do you? I want to help you find the true you. Sometimes, we get so bogged down in what others think about us that we pretend to be who they think we should be or act the way they think we should act. Well, it's time to free ourselves and start becoming the person that we were made to be. We can achieve that by simply knowing ourselves.

No one totally understands you. Yes, we have best friends,

relatives, siblings, pen-pals, or online acquaintances, but no one is inside your head like you are. There are some things that strap us down as an adult that has come from our childhood. Our first introduction to life is through our parents' eyes, our mother in particular, and then our father. God has designed us in a way where we depend on special care to survive. We are not like animals or primates. Take the sea turtle for instance, which lays their eggs on a dark sandy beach and leaves never to return. The baby turtles must fend for themselves, and in most cases, only 2% will survive from the clutch. We humans are born so vulnerable that we need constant care and physical touch, or else we would die. We aren't equipped with claws, teeth, or able to walk or even have the muscle capacity to hold our heads up without assistance, and feeding ourselves is out of the question. Some can manage most of those essentials earlier than others, but the reason the law sets the adult age at 18 is that we cannot be left to our own devices. We can't survive early on physically for years, so imagine how long being mentally capable would take. For at least 18 years in some aspects, we aren't able to take care of ourselves genuinely, so we need our parents. We need our mothers to nurture and feed us and our fathers to protect and provide for us. It's a team effort, and as a baby, we have no clue about life other than; we need food, comfort, warmth, love, and need our diapers continuously changed. As we grow, we come to understand things about life and how to operate in a family setting. We learn how to get things we want by asking or to earn things we want by doing. Not just physical things, but how to get our emotional needs met as well. We learn early on that; to get the respect, we must first give it, and to be trusted, we have to prove ourselves trustworthy. These things are learned by observation of our parents. If you see your parents constantly fighting, more than likely, you'll learn to resolve your problems in the same way. If we hear our parent's structure sentences and use phrases in a particular way when talking to each other, the chances are we will mirror those same antidotes. Earth is an ever-learning campus, and the subject is life. We, as students, are on a continual course of constant research so that we can be fully prepared for any test that it gives. We learn how to deal with hurt, pain, and disappointments by going through it. As we continue to grow, we try to minimize those hurts and disappointments by avoiding or by not allowing ourselves to be in the position to be hurt again. That's not always the right thing to do as we transition into adulthood, but mentally we haven't learned how to deal with rejection. Tic toc, tic toc, time to face problems head-on, learn from them and move on. Brushing an issue under the rug or to ignore it only compounds the problem. It will eventually be forced to come out, but at that time, it will not be controlled and usually under some type of duress. For example, if you are the type of person that hates confrontation, research suggests that you may avoid confrontational people and job careers that require confrontation, i.e., police officer, boxer, public debater, etc. If this person learned how to deal with confrontation instead of avoiding it entirely, they wouldn't be so limited in what they can and cannot do in life. Not dealing with your issues as a youth can determine your future in more ways than one. It can lead to bad relationships, dead-end jobs, and un-influential social circles. Parents can assist or advance children with their fears and anxieties early on, and without their parents, it'll be very difficult for children to navigate through life, bearing fears that never were addressed. Some of today's adult fears and social anxieties can all be traced back to what went wrong at home and who was or was not there to define them.

As a child, we mimic others and do what adults around us do, whether it's from our parents, our mentors, teachers, coaches, television, social media, or the congregation at church. Children tend to model the actions rather than the words of adults. When they move into their teenage years where they either rebel against or fall right in line with the system they'll only do it for the sole purpose of becoming something or someone they are not. First, let's ask the question, why? Why do we act the way we act and choose the friends we choose and work the jobs we work? Is it all by chance? Or does our childhood and how we were raised have anything to do with it? I've put together a memoir of observations, one on one sessions, life's experiences, meetings, and dealings with individuals that question who they are and why. If you took a survey or my challenge and ask twenty people, "Did your father play a major part in your life?".Most people will answer, "Yes," whether it was in a positive way or a negative one. They would all agree or conclude that their fathers' presence or absence made them the person they are today.

Why would a parent who was raised in a verbally and emotionally abusive home rage at their own kids? Why would a woman abused as a child marry a violent man? How does a teenager, sexually abused as a child, get drawn into a life of prostitution? Why does a man, beaten regularly as a child by his father, tend to be abusive to his own children? Wouldn't it seem that as an adult, one would be free to choose a better life for themselves and their children? From the outside looking in, it's hard to imagine that a person who endured such pains of abuse would abuse others, but oftentimes, this is the case. Children mimic what they see. While society's definition of an adult doesn't start until you stop acting like, talking like, and behaving like a child, you are still under the mindset of a child until you put those childish things behind you. Given these points, it's not too unimaginable that a bullied child would go on to bully others. Carrying emotional injuries from dysfunctional homes create deep wounds, and the results are often more powerful than the choices or desires of the afflicted.

Home Sweet Fatherless Home

We are of the age where each one of us is trying to figure out what went wrong. Why do I like the things I like? Why do I attract the people that I attract? Why did I choose this career? Why do I feel the need to be married or single, or to have kids or not? All these things are answered in our childhood. The events we experienced as children have had or will have a tremendous impact on our future. One thing is for sure and that's every person needs a mother and father. I'm not suggesting that people can't survive without one or the other, but statistics show that chances of success are better when you have both in your life. Being an adult takes molding and guidance. Every little boy needs his father to teach him how to be a man. Every little girl needs her mother to teach her how to be a woman. The lines get blurred when we began to eliminate the father from the equation. Same sex parents or single mothers can raise a child perfectly fine and show them all the love in the world, but that child will long for the guidance of a father figure. A substitute father can fill the shoes, but not the hole. The child will still want to know about their very own father. The where, the why, and the how come's will follow.

The answer to or the lack of information to those questions will greatly impact them for the rest of their lives. The heart of the fatherless is a formidable organ to navigate if the fatherless has not assumed acknowledgment that their heart was truly broken. When they are loved, they can sometimes reject the love offered because they do not feel loveable. When they're being supported, they reject that support because they do not feel worthy. At times, when they feel too comfortable in a relationship, they abandon it because of the fear of abandonment. It's all they know. Growing up in a fatherless home can be a traumatizing experience, but at some point, you are going to have to take control of your own life and take full responsibility for your own actions. Again, putting those childish things behind you. The first thing is to recognize that you were hurt by the fact that he abandoned you. No matter the reason for his absence, acknowledge that it has taken an emotional toll on you. The milestones and mistakes you're making today are probably generated from what you were and were not taught by your father. Many of our traumas can be traced back to our childhood. Of course, there is a myriad of other corresponding factors contributing to how our lives turns out, but the single most common denominator is our fathers.

For boys, a father can instruct his son on becoming a man and, ultimately, a father himself. Interactions between father and son are unique in that a father will emphasize the importance of responsibility in one's own actions as a man. So that when the day comes where the father isn't around to guide him, he'll make the right decisions that will ultimately protect him from harm. A father's wisdom leaves a lasting impression on a boy that he will carry with him throughout his life. At an early age for girls, a father is a foundation from which she can learn how to navigate the world, develop independence, establish self-esteem and build trust that won't be compromised in the real world. For both young boys and girls, without a father around, these things can still be achieved with the assistance of a stepfather, a close family member, or even various Big Brother programs across the nation. No matter how outstanding or phenomenal of a woman the mother is, it'll be a liability to that son or that daughter not to have a father there. The influence of a father is so powerfully permanent that the absence of one can be just as permanent, especially to a young person still in development.

I wanted to break this down to the very atoms of this subject and to do that, I must pose this question. What does a father mean to a child? When you're just a little person, trying to figure things out about life, like walking, eating, matching faces to things and things to places. The only people you know are your parents. These are the people that come to you when you cry, when you poop, and help you with everything you need. These are the only people you know. You hear their voices and match the vibrations of the soft one to your mother and the harder, more deep vibrations to your father. For a natural balance, we need them both. When the sound of that deep soothing voice is no longer around to send vibrations to your heart, you feel a loss. You long to hear it again. I compare this seeking, longing sound to the Emperor Penguins. Emperor Penguins live in the Antarctic far away from any predators and food alike, so they must trek back and forth out to sea to hunt for their food. When these penguins' mate, the pair leaves for weeks or sometimes months at a time. As a result, thousands of chicks practically identical to each other would huddle close together in groups called a crèche while the parents are away. When the parents return with a belly full of food, ready to feed their starving baby, they are bombarded by other hungry chicks begging to be fed.

The chicks don't care who feeds them; they're so hungry they beg from any passing parent. As the returning parent penguin waddles through hundreds of hungry, crying, desperate chicks, it cries out in each direction and listens for that familiar response. To the human ear, it all sounds like squawking noise. Instantly, the parent seeks out that unique sound, and the chick does the same. That sound is special and directly meant for that chick, and the chick must know to listen and respond to them both, mother and father. It's crucial to their survival.

All in all, the vibrating sounds that a human child listens for is profoundly distinct and designed just for them. When that sound is no longer around, the child notices and tries to fill it with everything else, but nothing fits. Only the father can make that sound, and only the child can recognize and receive it. A fatherless child, teen or adult, is that penguin chick squawking at every passing father figure crying out, "Are you my father? Are you my father?" searching for that missing familiar sound in response. Young boys cry out to men that may or may not be positive for them in their lives while young girls cry out to unworthy lovers that they feel are the missing man link to their lives. This shows up in relationships of the fatherless all the time. Where young women find themselves in one-sided relationships where they attempt to replace the sound of their absent fathers by dating a manufactured version of what was missing, fatherless men in relationships try to mimic what they believe a father should be. When people try to build their partners into something that was missing from their childhoods, it's a construction project that is built on quicksand and is bound to sink slowly. If, or rather, when that partner does not live up to the preconceived notions of those missing pieces, the relationship slowly sours.

I grew up in a time where fathers were the backbones of the family, the breadwinner, the leader, the patriarch. There are many books, movies, television shows past and present on the dynamics of a father-led family. The plots would vary but would take on social and economic issues that exist within a family. In entertainment television, the mother would always be the one showing patience, tenderness, and giving compassion, while the father would add supporting balance with his strength and guidance. These were the imagines shown through television and movies, but in the real world, we understood that sometimes, parents were unbalanced themselves, especially when the father was absent, tipping the scales of strength and guidance over to the mother. The father was defined throughout history as the provider, the disciplinarian, advisor, listener, and overall driving force in families. It was his role to be the source of income, strength, protection, and love. In his absence, a child lacks his guidance while growing up and will struggle. Most of the shows that you can research that doesn't have a father in the home, which aren't many, the children tend to struggle socially. If those shows could share a character breakdown on each of the children in those homes, the effects of an absent father would yield signs of depression. Since television is a make-believe world, slightly based on real-world issues, I can't assume that TV children would do poorly in school, be socially inept, or have depression based on their fatherless home. I can only assume that this can't be the outcome for all fatherless children. I wanted to find out all I could about the impacts of a fatherless childhood and how that could affect them in their adulthood. I began to do tons of research, conduct intimate interviews with fatherless children and adults.

Most of my research came from my time as a Camp Director of

Leadership camps for over 20 years. I had the chance to speak with hundreds of fatherless children and document their lives from childhood to adulthood and what I found was an epiphany to what I already assumed. A very high percentage had emotional and behavioral problems carried over from their childhoods. A smaller percentage showed some success when a substitute father was introduced early on in their childhood. When I began to re-read some of my interview notes and listen to my recordings, I felt a connection in the pain I was hearing as they told their stories. It raised my level of hurt, but it wasn't for them; it was for me. Personally, my biological father wasn't the one that raised me, but I never felt like a fatherless child because I always had a father in my life. So, my story was a little bit different. Or was it?

I stared at a blinking cursor, fingertips resting on my keyboard as I reflected on my very own childhood at this moment. When the computer screen went black, I saw my reflection as though I was looking into a mirror. I saw myself as an adult that I didn't recognize because I was thinking deeply about my childhood. Then I quickly realized that I've never really filled the hole in my own heart. I just camouflaged it with achievements and busyness. I still had unanswered questions that I needed to search for and things I needed to know about the father I never knew. Like, why didn't he search for me? Why did he leave, and most importantly, why didn't he want me? I peered deeper into my reflection and saw the little nine-year-old yearning for answers. I saw myself for the first time. I'm a grown-up with wounds from my past. Something's missing, but I don't know what it is. I feel like a normal person with work, school, relationships, and friends, but I still felt something was missing. A missing piece to my puzzle. Then as I fell deeper in meditation, I saw it... the hole that was missing was the relationship with my biological father. Who is he? What kind of man is he? Where is he? When I think about those things, it saddens me. I feel empty. I feel frustrated and alone. I feel abandoned and left to fend for myself like those baby turtles hatching on that dark beach crawling from that hole in the sand. How could this man leave me? I belong to him; I'm a great kid. As I sat in front of my computer, that emptiness widened in my heart. Nothing can fill that space, but him.

Answers from him or at least understanding of myself because of him. He is the hidden figure in my equation. I have a real father that raised me, loved me, protected me, guided me, and he is a wonderful dad; I wouldn't exchange him for all the money in the world, but there's something about knowing my biological parent. I can't explain the feeling, but it feels like a missing link in a chain that only one piece can satisfy. The hole in my heart is the size, shape, and outline of my biological father. As an adult, I had to figure this out through broken relationships, employment decisions, and socially with friends. I finally figured out how that hole in my heart affected me in my adulthood and how knowing this one thing has changed my entire life. I unconsciously carried that with me into every relationship, every thought, and decision I was making. How can I change that? How can I grow up on the inside? How can I grow up emotionally? How do I get closure on something that I cannot control? I can't get into a time machine and travel back to ask those questions or even go back to the last time I saw my biological father as my father. I can't, but what I can do is move forward with the solid information I do have and take control of my actions and my own emotions. I wanted to get the bottom of this thing that was holding people hostage from engaging and accepting what was and moving forward to what is.

Having my father step into my life was the ultimate blessing, but being abandoned by my biological father was the eventual reality. Growing up, I was intensely attuned to the attentiveness of others and the time they gave me. I keenly monitored closeness and distance in relationships, and to me, closeness meant to trust, and distance meant betrayal and abandonment. I had to learn to abandon that abandoned way of thinking and those abandonment behaviors. I found myself in a revolving circle of giving affection then taking it away in fear of being abandoned all over again. Falling in love and then sabotaging my relationship by retreating into withdrawal and isolation to protect myself. I would have a strong desire for intimacy, but then turn around and push that person away. It's a form of Affection/Withdrawal Behavior. The moment a woman began to reciprocate those feelings, I'd become afraid and subsequently would pull away emotionally. This pattern would repeat itself until the women became frustrated and conclusively leave. I'd justify it by saying, "See, she was gonna leave me anyway." or "I'm glad I didn't invest all of me into this or else I would've been so hurt right now." In my examination for answers, I've concluded that I was playing victim before there ever was a crime even committed. Having a fear-based way of thinking didn't work for me; I had to learn another way, and thank God I did. Teaching, training, and counseling children how to change the way they thought about themselves, at the time, didn't match up with how I was actually thinking about myself. I'm fully aware that it's inescapable what we do today affects our children and their children tomorrow. So, I had to do it for the future. I had to gather more information and more education to share with those that desperately needed it. Many abandoned adults are perplexed by how they treat social and romantic relationships as an impression of their feelings of abandonment. This is a testament to how the effects trickle down from generation to generation, and I want to help slow down or extinguish the abandoned mindset entirely.

There are a million children currently growing up without a father in the home today. Their absence has profound effects that can last well into their adult lives. Without a father's guidance and involvement, children can be susceptible to bullying, neglect, physical or sexual abuse, addiction, depression, and even experience suicidal thoughts ten times more than children with fathers in the home. It can jeopardize their emotional stability throughout their pre-teen and adolescent years. Even in school, studies show that a father's involvement with their kids has a higher likelihood of having better grades, but children with absent fathers struggle academically. A child needs the love of a mother and the guidance of a father. Together they build a more balanced adult but make no mistakes about it; neither one can be compromised without severe impacts on that child's future.

In a fatherless home, it can impact everyone involved. The children, of course, they feel abandoned, alone, and unwanted. The mother feels the impact because she is left to raise her children alone without the male counterpart or his support. And yes, even the father is affected. Although he's the main cause of the fatherless home, some would pose the question; How could he be affected when he's the cause of the problem? The answer could have been unforeseeable circumstances that kept him from the home; the main one that comes to mind is death, followed by incarceration and the awareness of knowing that he even had a child in the first place. These special circumstances have robbed our children of their fathers. Some would argue that, outside of death, that a father should still be responsible for his parental duties even when away from home. From 1960 through the 80's it may have been a harder task under some circumstances, but nowadays, we have advanced technology that allows us to be reached in all parts of the world, so there shouldn't be any excuse of a father not connecting with their child. Divorce, death, separation, incarceration, or inflation all modifies their ability to provide, which will ultimately affect the child throughout their adulthood when they feel left behind. We must remember that parents are fiduciaries to their children and fathers to their sons in particular because the father is the one that plants the seed of his son's character while laying out what it takes to becoming a man. The influence of a divorce, a separation, or even death, will affect a young boy’s own fatherhood as a parent. He may believe he's not needed to raise his own children because he didn't have one to raise him. Ritualistically, society has come to accept fathers as incapable of raising children when put up against the mother, and rightfully so, but his involvement is undoubtedly a positive benefactor to a child's development.

Consequently, all parties involved will be affected by a fatherless home. The mother, the father, and obviously the children. Each one has its own set of problems and will be forever changed because of his absence. My primary focus will be set on the children that are now adults that live with those changes. We live in a society with a considerably high number of fatherless children, and history shows that it monumentally affects their behavior. The Baby Boomers (born 1940-1960) had a formidable number of fatherless homes because many young fathers were drafted into war. Many didn't make it out, and others that came back were mentally broken and emotionally absent, they missed a lot in their children's lives. (Gen X 1961-1980) This generation had to deal with social and civil inequalities. There were welfare systems established, encouraging some lower to middle-class unmarried parents to stay apart for financial security, replacing the father's key attribute, providing for his family, coupled with social reforms. These systems secured entitlements and increased availability of benefits to families that were headed by women. Surprisingly, in the '70s, there was a slight increase in single-parent households headed by a single father. I suppose with governmental reforms in place men had to fight back to be with their children.

Fathers had to fight for their parental rights because mothers, by default, were keeping fathers away from the home in order to continue receiving welfare benefits. Read more on this at (www.theroot.com) The Millennial Generation, the generation born between 1981 and 2000, came up in a time where the fathers dealt with depression, alcoholism, and an influx of drugs, none of which were valid reasons to be absent from their children, however, it played a big part on the impending generation. No matter what degree or why the father left the home, fatherless children who are now adults feel a vacant emotion. With the advent of computers and web-based searching, children born after 2001, Generation Z, or Boomlets have a plethora of digital tools to find an absent father. Fathers to this generation cannot escape responsibility without the social media world finding out about it. Today's deadbeat dad will go viral for all the wrong reasons. I believe that we as a generation are getting better with raising our kids, even when the time has to be split between two parents. The problem with this new generational way of thinking is that people believe that parenting can be done singularly with no ill-effects to the children. The problem with this is that the outcomes won't be observable until early on in adulthood. By that time, any long-term effects have set in and may be too late to remedy. Although raising children by a single parent or same sex parent can be achieved, it shouldn't be a replacement model for raising children by both biological parents. A child needs the balance of both to have a more social and emotional healthier upbringing.

Make no mistake; thousands of functional adults have been birthed from fatherless homes that would tell you that they were emotionally and socially great growing up. Across nearly two decades as a counselor and educator, I question how great they "say" they are. I've worked with many people who grew up in a fatherless home, some accomplished, and others were restricted. The one common thread they shared was the fact that their father, not being in their lives, changed them. For some, it was a detriment to them and others, it was their driving force to beat the odds. The difference between the two paths they took rested on their thinking and how they perceived themselves. I found that the majority of the people I observed that went on to be emotionally stable were the ones that recognized and accepted the hole in their heart was caused by the emotion they attached to their absent father. They knew it was by no fault of their own and therefore avoided the feeling of unworthiness normally attached to abandonment. Instead, they filled that hole in their heart with goals and inspiration. They didn't waste time blaming themselves or feeling less than. They took that fatherless sour lemon and made sweet lemonade. Those are the unique situations because usually, fatherless children are at a high risk of educational difficulties, delinquency, unplanned pregnancies, underemployment, and or drug abuse. Whereas, their more low-risk peers from stable homes went on to live psychologically healthier lives, with supportive partners, better education, and lucrative careers. In early adulthood, they chose to seize opportunities that would move them forward in life, despite their absent fathers—becoming more confident adults. If more fatherless children tackled their emotions early on, they could avoid known and unknown unhealthy emotions. They would know the genesis of the emptiness they've experienced from time to time. Most adults don't realize fatherlessness affects them until they take the time to speak with someone, preferably a therapist, about what they believe to be a totally different set of problems. Many can't see it and don't obtain these discoveries until they have children of their own. Some will take it and make the best of their lives while others are bound by the debris that's left behind from their missing fathers. I wanted to know the effects fatherlessness had on a person in his/her adulthood and what separates those people from the rest. These are the consequences of the fatherless structure:

1. Single mothers usually have a hard time balancing work and child-rearing, which puts them in financial strains.
2. Drug and or alcohol abuse. Chemical abuse is 75% higher in adolescents from absent father homes.
3. Emotional health. Depression, anxiety, feelings of abandonment.
4. Education will suffer or be strangely successful.
5. Crime and delinquency will be higher.
6. Sexual activity, which raises the pre-teen pregnancy rate. (this is compared to homes with a strong father presence).
7. Suicide and suicide attempts are higher.
8. 80% of molesters and rapists come from absent father homes.
9. 90% are runaway children.

Many research and child development institutions share this list. i.e., the National Household of Education, Family and Youth Service Bureau, U.S. Department of Health and Human Services, and the National Center for Health Statistics. There is an unimaginable number of young boys and girls that are now adults feeling misunderstood. A vast majority of these stats are un-proportionately filled with inner-city youth. They run into a roadblock of their own emotions like resentment, hate, anger, regret, and guilt. I want to show them how to break through that roadblock and live a more productive and gratifying life. A portion of my decade-long case studies involving the effects of fatherlessness has shown to be synonymous with most, if not all, child and development institutions. The resentment, anger, anxiety, depression, and in some cases, hate that adults experience can all be attributed to being raised in a fatherless home. Fatherlessness doesn't always equate to abandonment. A child can be fatherless because of the reasons mentioned before, such as the death of a father, incarceration, employment, deportation, etc. Abandonment is the act of knowingly leaving your child. This can give a person a whole set of new emotional traumas that will be difficult to adjust from moving forward into adulthood. My focus will target the aspects of that physical and emotional abandonment. Let's take a closer look.

Physical abandonment is pretty obvious to define. It's when a child has been purposely left alone to fend for themselves, forgotten, cast away, forsaken, or deserted. This can diminish their self-esteem and give them a deep sense of worthlessness that can directly be related to being discarded. Physical abandonment leaves a child with a foundation of fear and loneliness that extends well into their adulthood. For young men, it can cause trouble with intimacy, whereas they don't allow people to get close to them. Afraid to form any kind of vulnerable connection with anyone because the fear of being abandoned in any capacity is intolerable. For young girls, abandonment invites trust issues that affect future relationships. For abandonment in general, being physically there for your child goes a long way. For a kid to look into the stands and see his/her parents there supporting them is paramount for that child's development. Sometimes parents can't attend every event, but those are the times where the parent should go overboard to hear all about what was missed. Being present when a child is speaking is also vitally important for their mental and emotional growth. To dismiss children or ignore them can be just as damaging to their psyche as being physically absent. Emotional abandonment can be equal to physical abandonment, to the tune of, it still gives off an undesired feeling of rejection, a feeling of being left alone, or discarded. Emotional abandonment makes a person feel at a loss, or cut off and deserted, ultimately causing them to withdraw. This form of abandonment occurs when the parent is physically present but emotionally absent. The father's focus can be distracted by work, relationships, drugs, or even other children from previous relationships. Although the physical needs of the child are met, there is no emotional intimacy developed from the father, no discipline, or male guidance.

A lot of touring musical artists find it hard to be physically home with their kids, but they become emotionally absent when they return because they'll begin new projects or networking with label execs, ignoring the emotional needs of their children. Children aren't invisible; they are not born into this world to be some sort of social status or human pet. They require attention, love, patience, and not simply heard, but to be listened to. They need feedback and guidance. They are not empty flash drives waiting for us to download general information, but delicate manuals that require individualized applications. Children know when a parent is not emotionally there; this emotional abandonment can and does have far-reaching effects well into their adulthood. Their emotional injuries need to be understood in for adequate healing because children who have been abandoned emotionally have a very good reason to fear abandonment as adults. They may not be able to verbalize those emotions of their parents' leaving and not returning, but those emotions are present. A shadow of despair and sorrow hovers that person who was left alone by the very people they trusted most and who were most important to them at that time in their lives. It's the fear of being abandoned again that births hurt, which manifests into loneliness and despair, which then turns into anger, ultimately causing a lifetime of resentment, if it is allowed to remain. No matter how many friends, likes, or followers they acquire or relationships they develop, the feeling never leaves them. As adults, they may not be aware that these emotions exist inside of them. Men have an easier time displaying that anger, and women have an easier time displaying the hurt, but there's an equal amount of hurt and anger in them both. As a child grows into his/her teenage years, with anger and hurt brewing deep inside, they feel that they must maintain tight control over their feelings. They learn to live with resentment, distrust, and sorrow. They hide it from the world. They've buried those emotions so that they could fit in and pretend to be like everyone else.

Children that were abandoned have an array of unfamiliar emotions and feelings at a very early age. They cannot define those emotions, so they tend to mimic the emotions from their mother's perspective on how to feel. In turn, they never truly address the hole in their heart or that ignored empty feeling. They just fill it with an emotional placebo. Frustration, guilt, mislaid love, animosity, or cynicism. They sample all kinds of emotions to see what fits. Some good emotions, some not so good, but never the less, they're temporary band-aids on a gaping wound that needs real therapeutic attention.

Children that are confused about how to deal with their emotions usually act that confusion out in other ways. This is where I run into all sorts of behavioral issues with the kids I counsel. I have seen this play out up close, and to be fair, children get a bad rap of being considered rebellious or out of control when parents don't understand them. The majority of the offenses are minor, but when their behavior gets an eyebrow raised, we (society) tend to go overboard with our punishment by sending the kid off to be someone else's problem. i.e., boarding school, military, boot camps, jail, to live with other relatives or to a doctor that will medicate their problems away. I have the perfect remedy to these problems, and this might seem too simple, but time and time again, I've watched it work, and that's listening. A child needs someone to give them time and listen to them from what they see, feel, and experience. They need an advocate and someone to empathize with them instead of being frustrated with them because we (society) don't understand them. 85% of their behavioral disorders originate from being raised without a father in the home. Without evaluating a child before attaching a standardized remedy, it will only momentarily solve the problem that will be doubling over time. Behavioral disorders are serious problems with the youth, and without knowing which disorder one has, it becomes difficult to treat. Here are a few: Conduct Disorders (hurting people and/or animals, stealing, vandalism, running away from home, skipping school, etc.), Oppositional Defiant Disorder (frequently arguing and being hostile towards authority figures, adults, and other children), Anxiety and Depressive Disorders, Attention-Deficit Hyperactivity Disorder or better known as ADHD. When the state of mental health in our children is ignored, we will soon have mentally ill adults with unresolved issues. These disorders speak to those who dealt with them on some level as a child, but now as an adult, there may be some underlying issues that this book can help define and relieve them from. Learn how to deal with problems with authority or how to keep your temper in check. Once you realized these foreign feelings could be the result of not having your father in the home while growing up, it could change your whole perspective on life. Even if you're now the parent that is in your child's life, your child will be growing up in a culture of fatherless children because of the effects it had on you. The effect is real. Fatherless children that are now adults themselves struggle to connect with their children emotionally in a healthy way. They are unaware of their own feelings and unable to express them appropriately, which puts love ones caught in a wave of emotions that was generated from childhood.

Most people can recognize the children that do not have fathers in the home because they were once that child or know one. These are the people who should become Big Brother's and Sister's, or be a mentor to someone they can relate to, understand, and assist in their development. There are people behind bars that never had the chance to be diagnosed and treated for any of these Disruptive

Behavior Disorders and possibly made choices that otherwise wouldn't have if the father was in the home. Considering that the vast number of children that end up in prison have some form of behavioral disorder. I want to share a story about this seven-year-old kid, Malik. I met him while volunteering at a YMCA in Compton, California. A rough neighborhood with a program for kids to keep them off the streets. I came from the same program myself as a youth, so giving back to this program was an easy choice for me. I wanted to find and mentor a child from my community. There were many great kids in the program, but the ones that I could help were the ones with behavioral issues. This kid stood out. He was always the center of any controversy. Whether it was child to child or an adult to child confrontation. This kid was a tough cookie. He didn't want to listen or abide by any of the rules. He seemed to have more on his heart than the others, and it was clearly, displayed in his behavior. He regularly claims innocence after being caught fighting or squabbling over games. He felt like the world was against him. He always had a reason for his part of the dissidence. When reprimanded, he'd lash out aggressively at the authority, dishing out the discipline. He'd curse, pout, ignore, cry, or flat out abuse anyone that stopped him from doing what he wanted to do. Despite his behavioral issues, he was a seemingly charismatic, eager, and honest about his feelings. He loved to talk and ask questions, but the only things he wanted to talk about most would be about the NBA and the players and their shoes. I would always speak to him and ask basketball related questions before asking him to do something I needed. Relating to children on their level on subjects they're familiar with was always my approach when dealing with troubled kids. Malik would tell me the stats of players and what they did in games. I was impressed with his knowledge of the sport at such a young age. Only if he applied that same focus into getting along with the other kids. I later found out that he was raised by only his mother, because his father was in and out of jail, so now I knew what I was dealing with. Malik wasn't the only child I counseled with one parent or the other in jail so I knew some of his make-up and what he must be dealing with. He wasn't my assigned kid, but I could see that his counselor couldn't manage him, and it frustrated her. Her way of dealing with him was to always set him apart from the other kids. One day my assigned kid didn't show up; he had a dental appointment, which gave me more time to assist other counselors with their activities. Just my luck, Malik was already serving a time-out for hitting another child. I asked his assigned counselor, Katie if I could work with him, and she happily agreed. We were in a small gymnasium, and he was in the far corner, fiddling with the wall. Looked like he was counting the bricks in the wall. He kept looking over his shoulder at the other kids on the opposite end of the gym having fun working on arts and crafts. I grabbed a basketball from the ball locker and began to dribble and put up some shots near him. He kept looking at me, I knew he wanted to play, but when I caught eye contact with him, he'd quickly look away. To get his attention I purposely rolled the ball off the back of his heels. He turned and looked at it then back at me. I asked, "So, what are in the corner for?" He didn't answer or acknowledged the ball at his feet. He just turned and planted his face back into the wall. "That's okay; you don't have to tell me, I already know." He stood so still that I thought he was a statue. I continued, "Yeah, Katie told me you were fighting." He folded his arms but didn't turn around and I didn't force him to. I grabbed the ball and continued to shoot jump shots. After a few more shots, I rolled the ball against his heels again. He turned and looked at it, and I told him, "I don't like it when people make me mad, I want to hit them too, but I don't because I'm strong. I'm strong on the outside with my muscles, but I'm talking about being strong inside. The person that doesn't fight is a person that is strong on the inside. Do you want me to teach you how to be strong on the inside? Are you strong?" Malik looks at me and nods, yes. "Katie says, you can play with the other kids after you get out of time out. Is that true?" He shrugs his shoulders. "Well, I told her if you can make two free throws, you can get out of the corner and join the others." He looked at the basket, and I tossed the ball in his arms. He was so small that I knew he couldn't make it from the free-throw line. So, I told him for every basket he missed, he has to tell me something about his home life. He agreed and took a shot. Air ball. He wasn't even close to making a basket, and I told him to move up and try again. He did and got ready to shoot. I stopped him before he could get off a shot and reminded him of the rules. "Now the agreement was if you missed, you would have to tell me something about your home life. You do follow the rules, don't you? Katie believes you don't, or at least you haven't proved it to her. I can tell her that you do follow the rules if you want me too. Would you like me to do that?" He nods, yes. I'm on a roll with this kid, getting him to open up to me. "So, tell me something about your mom?" He began to dribble the ball in place, and I can tell he was thinking. I repeated the question, he replied, "She at work." and reshot the ball, barely hitting the rim. I grabbed the rebound and held the ball. "Do you miss your mom when she's at work?" He nods, yes. "Yeah, I would miss my mom too." I toss the ball to him. He shoots again, and it banks off the backboard but doesn't go in. I collect the ball and ask, "What about your father?" He looked at his feet and took a beat. "The policeman took him." I gave him a bounced pass. "So, he's in jail?" He repeated, "Yeah, the policeman took him." Speaking with the others in the program, I already knew that his father was arrested for dealing drugs, and it was very traumatic for Malik. The sheriffs came early one morning, busting down his parent's door, pointing flashlights and guns at everyone in the home. He was terrified; he watched the officers rummage through his toys, searching for drugs, and barking commands. His father was taken away in handcuffs, while Malik cried hysterically throughout the whole ordeal. He was frightened, confused, and now scarred by that day he last saw his father. This particular program Malik was in was a way for single parents, mostly mothers, to get some help with their kids. Malik's mother worked a lot to cover the bills and usually left him with an adolescent family member to babysit while she was away. She tried hard to raise him, but she couldn't quite get past Maliks' disrespect and bad behavior, so she sent him to his Grandmother's house where he'd remained for over two years. At seven years old, he's showing traits of an abandoned child. I asked him, "How does your father not being at home with you make you feel?" He didn't even try to make the basket; he threw it hard against the backboard. "That wasn't even close, Malik. Are you upset?" He runs to grab the ball, but instead of picking it up, he kicks it further away. The ball rolls near the table where the other kids were, and one kid leaps from his chair and grabs the ball. Malik pushes him and takes the ball away. "Malik!" I run over. "That wasn't very nice of you." Malik began to explain how the ball was his, and he wasn't supposed to grab his ball. "It doesn't matter. Pushing and hitting isn't okay. Remember how we talked about being strong on the inside. That was outside strength, which always seems to get you into trouble. Let's use your inside strength next time by asking for the ball back first." He agrees. "Another way to be strong on the inside is to recognize when you're wrong and apologize for that wrong. Do you want to be strong on the inside? He agrees and then apologizes to the kid. To strengthen the bond with other children, I allowed those two kids to play with each other, shooting hoops. I noted small increments of progression with him throughout the summer, but I can tell his influences at home would counter that growth. Malik admired his drug-dealing Uncle, who was attaining temporary assets that held Malik's attention. Although his Uncle was a good person, he was a bad influence on him. Malik didn't care about his hustling on getting money. He only cared that his Uncle was present. This happens a lot in the fatherless community. Children will look for stability with other men, or take a 180-degree approach and reject men and their guidance entirely. Both decisions are fear-based. They'll attach themselves to someone that gives them security or shun them to avoid any possibility of being hurt. I constantly shared stories with Malik on what other kids of his age were doing and how much fun they were having, and maybe he'd like to do some of those same things. I knew he needed something else other than what he was getting at home, but that something else would require time and patience. Over the next few summers, his attendance lessoned to eventually none at all. Years later, I found out that he didn't graduate from high school but did complete his GED in a California Men's Correctional facility and picked up a welding trade. He fathered two kids of his own, secured a steady working job in construction, and broke the destructive cycle for his kids. I wouldn't outwardly prognosticate he had to go down that road before man'ing up, but those things he went through, in part, aligns with not having a father in the home.

Constructing this book took years to formulate because I had to see for myself the outcomes of some of the kids that I've observed. Malik didn't go to college, but I could have made that fair assumption of why back then. Only because children that live in father-absent homes struggle academically in school. Over 70% of high school dropouts are from fatherless homes, which significantly weigh on the child not attaining academic and professional qualifications in their adulthood. But a father's involvement with his child has a much higher likelihood of better grades; therefore, better education and more likely lead to a better professional career. I must pose the question; does a fatherless home keep children from becoming successful adults? The answer lies within that person, but it does make it more difficult for sure. Their adult life and the potential to reach their full capacity can be handicapped by the lack of a father's guidance, coupled with other corresponding pressing circumstances. Social scientists have shown that surprising patterns among those whose early lives reflect fatherless homes are at risk of educational woes. Many draw strengths from these difficult circumstances and see their struggle against it as one of the keys to their educational successes. Of course, there is enormous variability in terms of how individuals respond to adversity, and overcoming life's obstacles is hard in itself, but to know where it all generated from is the key to your change. There are many examples of men and women who rose to great heights without the support of a biological father.

They used what they didn't have to propel them to have it all. They took the attitude of "I had no father around, but I'll always be around for my kids." Although Malik's story was a turbulent one at best, I still applaud him that he took the higher road in flattening the curve of a fatherless generation. Malik is one of the thousands of children that had to grow up fast because their fathers consciously or subconsciously abandoned them. Sometimes in this exhilaration of maturity, it creates a baggage of issues that later on, needs to be sorted out. For that abandoned child that becomes a teenager who had been hurt by the people who were supposed to protect and love them may spend more time thinking more of death than life. That teenager soon becomes an adult, laden with unique stressors with trust issues. Those adults who thought they were unlovable and unworthy now have difficulties in romance. Sabotaging relationships and leaving those who try to love them broken in their path. Truthfully, they're simply adults who need to be reset. To do that, they'll need to revisit their childhood with full disclosure. Recognizing and verbalizing what happened to them as children. Face it, define it, and then discard it. Here lies the growth.

Absence makes the heart grow fonder? Says who? I've always wondered about that quote. Who wrote it, where did it come from, and most importantly does it relate to missing dads? When it comes to lovers, absence strengthens the bond because of all the memories they shared and currently missing. Concerning their absent fathers, the fondness will never grow, only the pain. In his absence, many unwanted feelings and emotions begin to sprout like weeds through the cracks of city sidewalks. Unwanted needs penetrates through even the most rigid of skin and eventually shows itself. An absent father carves out a hole in the heart, which leaves an outlined silhouette of a person unknown. They grow up feeling something's missing.

Who's my father? What was he like? Am I like him? Is he like me? If those questions are left blank, unanswered, and empty. That emptiness can be replaced by depression, suicidal thoughts, resentment, anxiety, and anger. Those emotions can and will bleed into parts of one's life without any warning. You can all of a sudden feel unworthy to work a job that you were clearly qualified for but have doubts which cause you anxiety and fear. Occurrences could pop up in your relationship, whereas abandonment has given you fear that your spouse will leave. Your defense mechanism to this fear has taught you to smother them with love or sabotage the entire relationship. You were forcing them to go under their own doing instead of being abandoned by them. All these things are a result of deep-rooted issues derived from your childhood and more so from not having a father in it.

There was a 1990's sitcom called "The Fresh Prince of Bel Aire," starring Will Smith as Will. He was the main character on the show, and each episode started with a reminder of his rough beginnings detailed in the opening theme song. Like many other African American teenagers living in close proximity of each other in low income, high crime communities, he was getting into all types of trouble and needed some quick discipline and structure. Prompting his single mother to send him off to his Aunt's house in Bel Aire, California, to save his life, hence the television theme song. In a study from the National Longitudinal Study of Adolescent Health, data revealed the number of fatherless homes in a neighborhood is low, and acts of teen violence will be high in that neighborhood. So, the character Will found himself in revolving violent situations. And without his mother's awareness to remove him from that environment, the likelihood of jail or death was imminent in his teenage future. The show ran for six years, tackling a myriad of serious topics with comical undertones. On one particular episode, Will, the Fresh Prince, is reunited with his biological father. He was reluctant to meet up with him at first because Will never forgave his father for leaving him and his mother. No goodbyes, no letter, no note, he just disappeared. This affected Will's youth and his decision making tremendously, which is why he found himself in constant trouble back home in Philadelphia.

Will eventually let his father back in, and for a couple of days, they begin to rebuild the bond that was lost during his childhood. Being with his father made a positive impact on him immediately. Will was a happy go lucky child again, and it reflected in his behavior. His father tells Will that he'll be leaving soon and want to take him along. Will was excited and felt like a kid again (Peter Pan Syndrome). He took no time to contemplate leaving the safety of his Aunt and Uncles stability to be with his flighty father. His Uncle Phil wasn't sold on the idea and didn't want to see Will get hurt again, so he scolds Will's deadbeat father and gives Will a bit of a warning. That doesn't go well with Will, because if there was any chance to be with his father again, he was going to take it, even if it hurt the family that grew to love and protect him. His Uncle thinks that Will shouldn't assume that his father will keep his word by taking him along. He reminds Will of the false expectations his father has built up in the past and warns him to be emotionally cautious. Will was so engulfed in the fun times he was spending with his absent now present father that he takes his Uncles warnings as jealously and controlling. In a heated exchange, Will stands up to his Uncle, the only father figure he ever knew, and told him, "To Hell with what you think, you're not my father!" This is something that deeply hurt children will feel throughout their years towards any authority figure that tries to give them unwanted guidance. When abandoned children feel pressure and emotionally hurt, they will use that same statement to disable and hurt whomever they really in actuality respect. Will's words cut his Uncle deep, and he's left dumbfounded. His Uncle can only imagine the whirlwind of emotions Will must be feeling over this man that's practically a stranger to him.

As the scene plays out, Will is upstairs getting a bag together to start a new life with his father. Downstairs, his father shows up, he and Uncle Phil have words. Will's father came with bad news. He can't take Will with him and wants to run out again without saying goodbye. Uncle Phil tells him that he won't let him off that easy this time. He'll have to tell Will himself. Uncle Phil adds, "...Will is not a coat that you hang in the closet, then pick it up when you're ready to wear it. His life goes on. He's not supposed to be here for you, you're supposed to be there for him." Will's father stammers to explain his sudden exit, but Uncle Phil doesn't buy his reasons and tells him that his son deserves to hear this lame reasoning from his father.

Despite Uncle Phil's stern advice, Will's father decides to leave without saying goodbye. Just then, before he could exit, Will comes bouncing down the staircase with a big smile on his face, happy, filled with anxious joy, and childhood excitement. Will's father is taken aback but knows he must now face his son and tell him the disappointing news. This scene was so hard to watch for many viewers because they related to being disappointed by someone they deem trustworthy too. Many tears fell on the night this episode aired. Will's excitement was quickly deflated upon hearing the news that his father wasn't taking him along and abandoning him again. The blood rushed out of Will's face, and it became cold as he listened. He stared right through his father's eyes as he tried to hold in his disappointment. He didn't want to give his father the satisfaction of seeing him unfold, so he tried to laugh it off, "Nah, it’s cool..." He says. Throughout the episode, Will has been referring to his father as "dad or daddy." With a straight face, he made it a point to call his father by his first name. "...I understand...Lou." Without another word said, his father turns and leaves. Will watches him go and holds his look towards the door as if he was still there. Will was seeing his father abandon him all over again.

UNCLE PHIL - I'm sorry, Will.

Will deflects with a smile as he whips around.

WILL - Ya know, actually this almost works out better for me, with the summer coming, the girls come to class wearing close to nothing, ya know what I'm sayin'.

UNCLE PHIL - Will, it's alright to be angry.

WILL - Why should I be mad? At least he said goodbye this time. I just wish I hadn't wasted my money buying this stupid present.

Will pulls a small statue out of his bag that he had planned on giving his father as a surprise. Then he slams it down on the coffee table. Uncle Phil tries to console Will's pain.

UNCLE PHIL - I'm sorry if it was something I could--

WILL - Hey, you know what, you don't have to do anything, Uncle Phil. It isn't like I'm still five years old, it ain't like I'm going to be sitting up every night asking my mom when daddy coming home. Who needs him? He wasn't there to teach me to shoot my first basket, but I learned, didn't I? And I got pretty darn good at it too, didn't I Uncle Phil? I went on my first date without him. I learned how to drive. I learned how to shave. I learned how to fight without him. I had fourteen great birthdays without him. He never sent me a damn card.

Will turns back towards the door his father just left out of and screams.

WILL (cont.) - THE HELL WITH HIM!

Will's breathing becomes quick. He's hurt. He then turns back to walk out, pass Uncle Phil.

WILL (cont.) - I didn't need him then, and I don't need him now.

Uncle Phil tries to console him, but Will jumps back as if he doesn't want to be touched.

Will (cont.) - You know what, Uncle Phil, I'm going to get through college without him, I'm going to get a great job without him, I'm going to marry me a beautiful hunny, and I'm going to have me a whole bunch of kids. I'm going to be a better father than he ever was. And sure, as hell don't need him for that, cus there's not a damn thing he could ever teach me about how to love my kids!

Uncle Phil and Will, looking at each other face-to-face. This tough street kid from Philly for the first time in his life breaks down. Tears roll down both cheeks. Then soft and broken.

WILL (cont.) - How come he doesn't want me, man?

Will collapses into Uncle Phil's waiting arms, and they cry together. Season 04 Episode 24.

Emotionally bruising stories about fathers and sons and the love they can give or deny makes for good cinema. Will was denied his father's love, which caused him to be a menace to society, and led his mother to send him away. Will's father never had a father in his life, so he really had no clue about what to do to be a father. It was evident throughout the episode when he was taking his adult son to kiddie carnivals and playing childish games. i.e., trying to make up for lost time. Time can't be put back on the clock, so you can only make use of the time you have now. Will was broken, even with a stable father figure and a supportive family that loved and embraced him, he still longed for the love of his father. That longing has altered his behavior as a teenager, and if the show could continue into his adult years, we as viewers would witness the reflection of his traumatized childhood. Although Malik and Will's stories aren't too far different from each other, they parallel in many ways. One of which was the influence of a father figure, their uncles that changed their lives. They both had behavioral disorders, both didn't do good in school, both went to jail at one point, and both held resentment towards their biological fathers. The origin of it all in both was the absent father.

I'm not implying that fatherless adults are flawed or even that adults that had fathers in the home are not, but rather, to say that overcoming the mental and emotional effects of fatherlessness is a choice to be made. I would hardly consider growing up fatherless to be a desirable position to hold. Yet, many who grew up without a father do say that they have benefited in precisely this way. For example, the police officer who was bullied in his youth felt it necessary to become a protector of children who couldn't protect themselves. Or the judge, who grew up fatherless himself, wanted to change the lives of youth that came before him by issuing out tough love to redeem the lives of the misguided generation ahead. They filled the holes in their hearts by studying more and becoming something of themselves. Those who believe they've made independent decisions despite their fatherless upbringing resist defeat and the stigma and stain of not having a father around in their lives. Perfect example; Shaquille O'Neil and Stephen Curry, both accomplished professional NBA players with multiple MVPs and World titles between them. The world would consider them very successful. They both are family men, both are loved by millions, both are well-rounded citizens, but what they don't share was who raised them. Shaquille's father left when he was young, not too different from many other NBA/NFL players with similar storylines. Fortunately for Shaq, he had a wonderful man step into his life with discipline, guidance, and structure. Shaq never hated his biological father but wrote a rap song entitled, "My Biological Didn't Bother" He seemed to find the strength to fuel his success with his fathers' absence. Simultaneously, Steph Curry's dad was there every step of the way with the same guidance and structure. With this comparison, you can see how Shaq used his fatherlessness to fuel him to be the best he could be regardless of his absent father. He's a great dad to his very own children and the opposite of what his biological father lacked in contribution.

When life inevitably becomes difficult, we must remember that we have the power to change and begin to fill that hole with knowledge, skills, love, and progression. Be bold and face adversity, then defeat it, continue to remember the ways you've overcome adversity, and repeat it. Suppress those negative emotions that keep you in a constant loop of self-doubt and be courageous in your approach to life, because it will be an ongoing battle of suppression. Whether it's through studying harder or loving yourself more, just remember you can't win if you allow yourself to stay abandoned. We often remind ourselves of what has gone wrong in our lives rather than what we did to overcome those emotional and mental challenges. Give thought to the filled portion in the emptiness of your heart rather than the empty space that needs to be filled. It has become a significant problem for those adults that linger on the latter. Some adults have learned and developed attachments, which is simply an emotional bond with another person. These attachments affect our subconscious assumptions about the world as we see it and how those assumptions influence our adult relationships. So, where did these attachments that formed our personalities come from? Is it from friends, our teachers, coaches, priests, or pastors? It all depends on your parents and what they bring out of you. The person that you were raised by can determine how you turn out as an adult.

We as adults, through our attachments, develop characteristics and ways to connect with the world, our perceptions, trust, and dependability to others, all based on the upbringing with our parents. So, what kind of parents did you have? Did you have parents who weren't consistently available? Slow to respond to your needs, perceptive but detached? These types of ambivalent parents give children contradictory feelings and create a character of anxiousness, and needing constant reassurance, always looking to others for their worth. What about parents who were frightening and often displayed disapproval or anger towards their children? You know, the parents that you feared. Growing up, I had a buddy with the scariest mom ever. She lived in a corner house at the end of our block. It made it convenient for us to cut across her grass instead of using the sidewalk. If and when she would catch us, it would be hell to pay. We dared stepped on her grass if she was home or climbed into her backyard for lost baseballs balls. She was a single parent and always seemed to be angry, yelling at the kids in the neighborhood for practically anything. I even think she got mad at us one time for breathing too loud while we took naps. This type of parent would often cause a person to be chaotic and confused. As an adult, this could manifest as being hot and cold in relationships, pulling others toward them, then inexplicably pushing them away. Parents that were emotionally unavailable and unresponsive would cause a child to be fearful of rejection, and they would tend to avoid intimate relationships with others. These children may grow up to appear self-sufficient and independent, but that appearance is usually camouflaging a more profound fear of rejection and abandonment.

Children's relationships with their parents shape their social, emotional, and cognitive development, and there are links between how children are brought up and the parents that raised them. That affects their will to be either well-adjusted or maladjusted adults. Our parents can leave an imprint on our lives early on that can be good or bad. Wait, what's an imprint? An Imprint is a fixed memory, a lasting impression, effect, or influence. An Imprint is like a recalled memory, and we play it over and over as we grow to which we form relationships, friendships, and partnerships. We must take time to realize what our Imprint is and use it to our advantage or delete it from our memory files entirely. Knowing about your Imprint memory gives you the tools to free yourself from the past. For the purpose of this book, I'm going to re-name Imprint to Fragments of Memories, because that's what it is. We keep these memories in our brains and recall them whenever we are cornered with difficulties. Life is a series of reactions to the most recent event. We react to them with only knowing what we know from our fragments of memories to how we felt when last threatened. Depending on the individual, the choices we make in that reactionary period could be detrimental or inspirited to their lives. Choose wisely

Where Do the Blame Lie?

THE PARENTS, a child's first line of defense against the world, but also the first ones to blame when things go wrong as an adult. When a child misbehaves in public, society tends to point the finger at the parents. They get the blame for not adequately equipping their children for societal challenges at home. There are some adults out here still blaming their parents for their actions or the lack thereof. At some point, you will have to take full responsibility for the actions you take. There are unique factors that play a part in individuals and who they are today, such as environment, attachments, and fragments of memories we spoke of in the last chapter, but now it's time to take responsibility and control of your own life and be who you choose to be, not who you think you are.

Are parents the blame for fatherlessness? Absolutely because the partnership between the parents together forms the entity that is you, they share the responsibilities of nurturing, loving, caring for, instructing, and protecting any children that they bare. To be fair, no one is formally taught to be a parent, unless you count playing house while growing up with siblings or neighborhood kids. Many parents instruct with learned behaviors that were passed down to them. If their parents made them work for an allowance, then that parent will more likely make their kids work for an allowance as well. If their parents always fought in front of their children. There are chances that they will do the same in the presence of their children. Most of their behaviors will be learned from their parents. Some from their mother and some from their father, it's a balance. I clearly understand that we live in a tech-driven world today, social media era, so it's not surprising that parents of old have different opinions about child-rearing than parents of the new. Generations differ widely in their life experiences, values, and what's socially acceptable, in such, so does that generation's way of teaching. What doesn't differ is our childhood to adulthood connection; what's taught as a child will impact us negatively or positively in our adult life. For better or for worse, if the parents decide to separate, customarily, the mother will retain custody of the children. With this, the mother will have a greater influence over them. Subsequently, if the father decides not to be a part of his ex-spouses' life, by default, the child will be affected and will experience signs of abandonment. Perhaps most significantly, the earlier the stages of separation are, the more damaging the effects will be. We must remember the main purpose is to raise children so that they are happy with themselves and can take care of themselves when the parents aren't around. With the overwhelming number of children and young adults living with abandonment issues, there's a pretty high chance that even responsible parents will be raising their kids in a culture of fatherless children. A culture of angry, misguided, depressed boys and confused, resentful, always searching for love young girls. For many parents, the problem is the lack of rules, and for others, it's the ability to enforce them. Parents have to figure this out early on, or else they will have children that lack discipline and not only be a problem for the parents, but they'll be a problem for society. At first glance, we can set the entire blame on the laps of the parents because it was their independent individual decision to leave the family structure, not the children.

Let's meet this fatherless assemble and examine each separately, starting with the mother. The mother is the one that the child would turn to for emotional and spiritual guidance. You may ask yourself, how does the mother share in any of the responsibilities of a fatherless environment set for her child? Let's be honest; if she doesn't make the right choices in a partner, it can hurt the wellbeing of her children, physically, emotionally, or mentally. Entertaining and choosing a drug addict, seasoned criminal, or even an unprotected one-night stand are all examples of poor choices from the beginning. Of course, I'm swinging to the obvious end of the pendulum, but it's still a part of the pendulum. Society will criticize her when her kids develop behavioral issues because of his absence, but this is misplaced. How can she be the blame for him not being a father to their shared responsibility? As-how unfair as it seems, society will look to her for all the answers. Before I continue, let me set an important personal disclaimer: I believe it's imperative that we understand the concern, pains, and anguish that mothers experience as they attempt to raise their children, sons in particular. I want to personally and gratefully give thanks to all of them. We are all forever indebted to mothers, and we should give them the utmost respect for being deliverers of life. Without the mother, we wouldn't have anything. At times, a mother may feel as if it's a never-ending chore, yet still do it effortlessly for nothing in return but love. The sweetest thing to me next to Jesus is a mother. With that said, there are circumstances, forced or otherwise, to which a child can become fatherless by way of the mother's actions. Single parenting by choice is something that shouldn't be a choice, but sadly it is. These are women that choose to become pregnant but have no desire to be with the father. Others may choose adoption because they feel their biological clock has run out of time while searching for the right partner. In other cases, a woman is unable or unwilling to have children independently and may choose surrogacy with her same-sex partner. In this case, by default, the children are fatherless from conception. Some would argue that even without a father, the child will be just fine. There are debates amongst experts as to the important components of what the family structure is. Whether it's centering on step-parents, same-sex partners, foster parents, etc. Is it more important than the love and affection of the children's biological parents? Some believe that as long as the child is loved and taken care of, that they will be balanced, and well. Although this thinking is honest, it's incorrect; the child will always feel the absence of their father. By way of other children with fathers, social media, television, friends at school, or just a burning desire to know. Studying young adults for over 30 years, I see that the ones that were raised by single mothers are doing satisfactorily, though distinct minorities are having some problems. That minority is the majority in many black and brown communities. Having a father in the home is ultra-important to a community that is already laden with social and economic issues, but I've digressed. Let me get back to who's to be the blame for a fatherless home. I want to be clear that it's not necessarily who's to be blamed more, but rather how it came to be. The choices made or the decisions that were set forth that caused a child to be fatherless. Women have a lot of power over choice, and their choices are what set the premise for most of what makes a family. A woman can have a child and title themselves mother, but a mother is one who will put their child above their wants and needs. So, I ask, is it a want or a need to leave their child's father? Some would answer, depends on the circumstances. And there could be many. I would counter, what about the mother who wanted a baby more than she wanted the relationship? The mother that laid with a man solely for financial gain? The mother that tried, but could not make the man step up to his responsibilities, so she traded him in for another man and subsequently, another father for her child. I'm speaking of the mother that gladly and sometimes preferably takes on both roles of the mother and the father. The mother pleads for the biological father to see his kid with no success. The mother that simply made a bad decision on copulating with this dead beat in the first place. Is she to be blamed because the relationship didn't work out? Some will say, "Well, she chose him." and "You made your bed, now lay in it." and others would say, "You don't have to stay in the relationship that isn't working to raise your child.". In cases of unintended pregnancies, it creates a fragile family infrastructure. So, in that case, is it the mother's fault? There could be many more scenarios for a mother leaving the father; abuse, rape, incarceration, or deaths of the father are some of the exceptions where the choice was taken away from the mother. She couldn't have known that the man would be abusive, or die, or was struck with some serious disorder that restricted him mentally of taking care of his children. In those cases, the mother is clearly, free of blame.

Today's society tells us if it doesn't work, walk away. Life is too short, and why stay in a situation that you didn't sign up for? Again, it's a choice. Choosing another mate isn't the same as choosing another father for your child. Children cannot choose; they are bonded by blood to the man that made them. No matter the circumstances or scenarios, they will feel the effects of said change. Clearly, the mother can't be the blame for a father not coming around? That's his choice. But the questioned I posed was, does the mother share in the fault of a child's fatherlessness?

In some cases, yes. It boils down to choices and putting the child's wants and needs above the mother's wants and needs. But you may add, if the mother isn't happy, then the child won't be happy, and why stay in a terrible relationship and allow the child to witness a mother and father fighting or not loving each other? Again, those are the choices of the mother to dissolve toxic relationships, not the children. If we're being totally honest, all the fatherless relationships weren't toxic. It just wasn't what the mother wanted; she may wish to have a man with more money or for him to have more affection or more anything. Those are her wants, not the children. You may say the child will benefit in the long run, but in the short term, the emotions are being built, and the disorders are being developed. There will be a time where the mother will have to answer three things for the child without his father. Where, why, and what? Where is he? Why didn't he stay and what happened? If the child's age isn't appropriate for this dialogue, then save it for a later date, but by no means lie or embellish the truth. This tends to hurt the relationship between the mother and child. Children have trouble with their absent fathers because of how their mothers defined him, making it understandable. The child will hear that story over and over in their head like a boomerang filter, stuck in a constant replay. If the mother feels she can no longer delay the truth of why the father isn't around, she should say what's needed, like the love they both shared for the child was genuine, but the love they shared for each other was not, and things could not exist the way it was.

Softly say those hard things: He chose to leave us, I left him, he cheated, I cheated, etc. The mother should not lie to protect her or the father's image. Let the truth be the truth. The mother shouldn't believe she's protecting her child from the facts because, in the long run, it will hurt them and everybody involved, so it's best to be upfront and honest early on. Avoidance of it is also dangerous because if left up to the child to guess-timate, they may feel that he/she wasn't good enough and begin to question themselves, damaging their self-esteem. It is not solely the mother's responsibility to protect her child from the truth, but it is her responsibility to be transparent to the child that is owed an honest answer about his/her father. The truth will hurt, but the effects of growing up fatherless will be lessened with a better understanding of the three W's. 'The where, the why, and the what.'

Now, let's examine the culprit of all that's wrong in America, the absent father. Here are three examples of absent father excuses and why they left:

1. The first is the father that didn't want to be a dad in the first

place; I never wanted kids. It was a one-night stand, the condom busted, she was a gold digger and trapped me, she said she was on the pill, I can't afford a baby, I was drunk.

2. The second is the father that had good intentions going in, but the relationship wasn't based on solid ground, so it fell apart; He tried being there early on when he separated from the mother, until she started dating someone else. She made it difficult for him to see his kid because of whatever reason, and he didn't want to be controlled, so he fled.

3. Then there's the father that never knew he was a father to be; That's not my baby; I was overseas in the military and didn't know. She didn't tell me. etc. etc. Even sperm banks or sperm donors fall under this last category.

Before I analyze these fathers' excuses, let's talk about how society sees the father. Society has come to accept fathers as incapable of raising children when put up against the mother, and for the most part, this is true. There's a special bond a mother has with a child than a father; it's just different in its own, special way. Never the less his presence is still needed when raising children. Generally, men are thought to be the breadwinners of the union and the women the nurturers. In a society that emphasizes that being a man meant being the breadwinner has dramatically changed. Even though work remains vitally important to a man's self-image, it isn't the only criteria that society grades him on, because nowadays, women are making just as much or more money than men. Traditionally children have been raised by women, both in the home and in schools. Women educators outnumber men in our schools and fatherless children would leave a female-driven home to go to schools where their teachers were women as well. The times they did get male interactions was when their mother would interact with one socially. Times have changed, men's involvement in parenting has stepped up since the '70s. and today there are more male educators with male-driven curriculums, but not enough. Men have split the workload and became stay at home dads, and the women were the breadwinners of the family. So, the lame excuse of men leaving their family because they feel that they cannot provide is a thing of the past.

Children need both parents, and today's parents equally contribute financially, and both parents assist in the rearing of the children to hopefully produce a well-balanced human being. What does it mean to be a good father? By society's definition, a father that meets his financial obligations, taking care of his children, and being the protector of his home. Who is the father? What kind of man would leave his family behind? One would surmise that no person could leave a defenseless child and mother to fend for themselves, but a lot of men have done just that. Who are they? Maury Polvick of The Maury Polivick Show has been asking that question for years. This long time, running television show centers around women searching for the fathers of their children. Maury interviews and tests the paternity of young men to conclude if they are or are not the father of children of the women they've slept with. "You are the father!" is his most famous coined phrase from the show. It's so fitting here because dead beat fathers use many excuses on why they weren't there for their children. It's drama-filled and perfect for day time television, but not so good for the children involved. It's a sad game that these parents play, and its unnecessarily time lost going back and forth on factual paternity. It's truly a loss for the child because it's that bonding time that can never be recaptured. Children are innocent and unaware of the problems that their parents are having. They desire love and affection and to be provided with food, guidance, and protection the entire time of their development. Men that sleep with women and then claim that the baby isn't theirs are the ones that are the true deadbeats. If there's any possibility that the child may be his, his first responsibility should be to secure that child's wellbeing. Paternity should be second if that's in question. Fathers that delay fatherhood because of paternity are the same ones that will delay child support payments. That's what it boils down to, to them. They don't want to be locked in a bond with the woman they laid with. And don't want to have anything to do with the child that came from it. That's not the child's fault, and it will be the child that suffers the most. On the other side of the coin, some fathers want to take care of their children, but don't want to deal with the woman explicitly. In these cases, it's always some dispute between the parents. The courts get involved, and it's a never-ending battle for custody. Men consider this paradox. Time is all that the child wants, and support is what the mother needs, whether it's in service or currency. These two things are a must to have to raise healthy children. Withholding either of those only makes it more difficult for the mother, the child, and the father himself. A father that doesn't pay child support loses common privileges such as; they're not allowed to travel out of the country, suspending certain driving and business licenses they've attained, garnished wages, and even incarceration. The fathers are all treated the same in the eyes of the court. The ones that refuse to pay and the ones that can't pay due to unemployment happenstances resulting from license suspensions. Not every absent father is absent by choice. There are some circumstances where fathers are denied access to their children because of their financial situations, these are forced father's absences. Vindictive women would say, "If he doesn't pay, he doesn't get to play with his child." That's the broken truth, it's not the money that raises the child it's the man. For the men that honestly want to be in their children's lives but are blocked by their finances are mentally and physically broken. One thing men desperately wanting to be with their children would tell me is that there's no greater pain that compares to the prohibitory access of seeing their children. Again, not every absent father is absent by choice. Studies show that 50% of divorced fathers have ex-wives that interfere with visitation with their child. Similarly, approximately 40% of custodial mothers admit denying their ex-husband visitation to punish him. That 40% of custodial mothers feel that they have no other recourse other than withholding the father's rights until she gets what she wants and needs. This is malicious and unlawful, to say the least against the father and, of course, an undeniable offense against the child. I'm acutely aware of the unmet financial obligations of these men and by no means am I aligning myself with deadbeat dads, but to punish the child because of the man's financial strains is cruel. It's vitally important for a man's psyche and self-image to take care of his family, and if and when that isn't achieved, it can severely damage his self-esteem. A father's financial situation is the measure in which a man feels about himself, and often in our society, a high value is placed on his income and the weight of his wallet. It may sound shallow, but it's the facts. Many women may not admit to it, but surveys show that 95% of women 21-40 agree that financial security is paramount in the choosing of a mate. Men understand this and strive to make lots of money to snag a mate themselves. Some men that do not have that earning potential focuses on other attributes that they may have, but still give the appearance of money or at least the ambition to provide for a possible family. When a man meets a woman, there's a natural selection process. She chooses based on a couple criteria's and one of which is earning potential.

So, when a man creates a family and feels that his finances don't align with what he believes is needed to have a family, he bails. Afraid to let everyone down, afraid to face the problems that will come, some say they don't want to be a burden to the woman and the child. A bruised ego and lowered self-esteem have overwhelmed him, and he mentally and physically bows out. These types of men that rationalize that way would rather abandon their families than to stay in a state of despair in fear of ridicule. This is a selfish way of thinking, but in their minds, they believe their child will be just fine. Some may even think and equate it to, "I didn't have a father when I grew up, and I turned out okay, so my child will be okay." This is terrible, and in these cases, the fatherless cycle has repeated itself. This type of man will come up with all types of reasons why he didn't stay or didn't contribute to the rearing of his child. None will be acceptable to his offspring or the mother. He is not thinking of his first responsibility, which is his children; instead he thinks about himself. We can debate this and add different scenarios to it, but the bottom line is that if the man makes the baby, he should take care of the baby no matter what it takes. It's his job and not someone else's. If it means making life-changing decisions nine months before the birth or nine years after birth, the child will need his/her father.

Fathers play an irreplaceable role in children's lives. They shouldn't expect the woman to raise children on their own. I like to ask young fathers that aren't in their children's lives, who are you? Meaning that, what kind of father are you? Who are you as a person? Do you value the cycle of life? I usually get answers that speak to them as they see themselves, but not who they actually are. I like to dig deeper into them and find out the thought pattern and the surrounding circumstances that made them make those choices not be a part of his child's life? It's a hard question for them to answer, but most will re-direct the blame elsewhere when in actuality, the entire fault lies with him; it was their choice. I would always urge fathers to do everything humanly possible, within the law, to be a part of their child's lives.

The only fathers that I hold exempt are fathers that have died or were honestly unaware that they were even fathers in the first place. Everyone else can or could have made an effort to be a part of their child's life. One may ask what about the fathers that are in jail or the military. How can they be the blame if they cannot see their children regularly? The jailbird and the journeymen, even though these two types of fathers are at different points on the parenting continuum, they both can still be great parents. Both fathers take up a vast portion of that child's life, and their presence or lack thereof will significantly affect their behavior and, by default, may exhibit traits of abandonment without actually being abandoned. The feelings of abandoned children aren't all the same, but there's one thing that's congruent with each, and that's the fact that the only biological father they have isn't around. Regardless if it was by force or by choice.

I remember at 18, I joined the Army and was stationed at Fort Dix, New Jersey, for basic training. Being away from my family for the first time was a real eye-opener to false independence. Thinking I was free of my mother's rule and on my own to do as I wanted. I was surprisingly mistaken. Strange men, barking orders, screaming, and yelling at me the minute I got off the bus on base. At the time, it was terrifying, but over a grueling eight weeks of training and self-realization, I learned to respect their authority because they exuded a form of discipline that I missed at home from my own father. My father worked a lot, and when he was home, he was a laid-back kind of dad, not many rules, but when he did make a rule, it was to be followed. I remember missing him a lot growing up and waiting for him to get home from days or sometimes weeks of being gone. Most of my parent-child interaction was seemingly with my mother. School meetings, baseball practices, ceremonies, and graduations were all with my mother. My father was the disciplinarian, but it only came when my mother ordered it. She was indeed the dictating Queen in our castle. Subsequently, having my father away in spurts added to my slight traits of abandonment.

Children that have fathers deployed in the military or fathers with work assignments that require months away from home will exhibit some signs of fatherlessness. Incarceration is more complicated, there are ways to be involved in your child's life from behind bars. It'll take an awful lot of support from the mother or guardian. As minimal as that may be, it's still something that the child can benefit from in the long run. Thereupon, if the mother doesn't assist in this, it's nearly impossible for an incarcerated father to be a part of his child's life; for this reason, is he the blame for his child being fatherless? Recurrently, it comes down to choice. I'd first ask what caused him to be behind bars? What choices were made that lead up to this predicament? Some absent fathers grew up without a father around themselves throughout their childhood. So I'd ask them about their father.

Lastly, I'd ask was writing, phoning, or visitation accessible? With today's technology, some apps are designed to connect inmates with families by converting text into handwritten letters. After those questions and answers were satisfied, I'd still conclude that he cannot be excluded from blame. My reasoning is that there were a series of choices that lead up to the incarceration and decisions made by him alone. So no, I can't give him a pass on his absentee because he's behind bars, but I'll have greater understanding of how his involvement was severely limited.

What about the divorced father? Is he blameless for his child growing up fatherless? Of course not, that's preposterous. Being divorced from your wife is not being divorced from your kids.

Divorcees must make every attempt to continue to be a part of their children's lives, even if the ex-wife is making it difficult to do so. Fathers feel they instinctively have no rights, while other fathers believe that the government is more interested in getting money than keeping families together. They believe that the system is hindering women by keeping them reliant on the welfare system instead of keeping fathers in the home. Divorced fathers complain about the unfairness they feel they received in the divorce court system and attribute alimony as a form of forced slavery. That's an extreme comparison, but they add that the creation of alimony has made lifetime daters out of their exes. It encourages women not to re-marry because, under alimony rules, the payments will cease if she weds. Some women will go as far as to keep their exes' last name to continue getting paid under their alimony agreement, even though they are in an entirely new relationship. Each situation is unique, and the reasons may vary, yet we must admit that some women take full advantage of these outdated laws and are unapologetic about it. Men want to pay a reasonable amount, but fathers can't make that decision. Only the courts can determine what's reasonable. The courts will measure it against the father's income and the families living expenses at the time of the divorce. Let's set aside the men's alimony complaints, and let's discuss the fact that children are used as pawns in this chess game of visitation. Fathers fight for more visitation rights, and women fight for more child support. It's an on-going topic among divorcees.

Fathers feel as though they can't be the parent they would like to be because of their exes' interference. They say that it's that frustration that keeps them away from being with their kids. It's not a valid reason to abandon your child, but it is a harmonious argument. Men that abandon their children because they do not want to deal with their baby's mother are a weak cop-out. That's one of the things that the family court was designed to do, set up visitations of the children for parents that could not figure it out on their own. If those visits aren't adhered to by the mother, do not punish the child by giving up. Fight! Fight for your rights. Fathers feel that as the child grows during these battles, there's an unfair resentment against him from the child, and that's a reason to stay away. Thinking they're making it easier for the child by shielding them from the drama. Untrue. Co-parenting is better than no parenting any day of the week. Baby Mama drama is just another complaint that abandoning fathers will use to dodge responsibilities. These fathers' experiences are not universally dismal; some groups of fathers have redirected their goal for their children and continue to be great fathers. What men have to do is separate alimony from child support. It's not the same, but the problem isn't just the division of the funds. It's how a man feels. He feels erased, and so goes his parental influence. When a man feels as though his only existence is to work and pay, essentially becoming a working wallet, they are resistant to either support, child or alimony. Damaged men will go as far as to attempt to hide earned income to avoid paying high child support orders to the women. (i.e., reasons why some women fight for more support) Men just don't want to be reduced to only a wallet or what some may call a Disneyland Dad. The dad who doesn't spend quality time with his kids, but spends money to show affection. In the stage play, later adapted into a movie, Fences. The father and head of the household struggles to provide for his family but makes it work. What he does have is strict discipline over his son. Later, the father admits to having an affair and fathering another family across town; this hurts the entire family. The mother kicks him out of the house, and with him goes the respect they had for him. In an emotionally driven scene, the son stands up to his father for the first time and tells him, "You don't count here anymore." When men feel as if their discipline and direction is no longer valid, they lack importance, and they either fight or flee to avoid the pain. In the case of abandoned children, they flee. Feeling more of a liability than an asset, these abandoning fathers believe that they've failed as fathers and begin to re-examine their role in the family structure and choose to disappear rather than face their family issues with humility and forthcoming adjustments to correct it. Back in the day, men used to abandon families all the time, and then create a fresh start with a whole new family on the other side of town. They felt they could do that because, in this new family, he's not a failure. The anxieties must have been expediential to just up and leave your family. Those men never stopped to think how hard it would be for her? She can't simply push a restart button. She has to deal with looming bills on top of the relationship's heartache, and societal judgments from friends, family and neighbors while trying to raise a child with tons of questions about his father's whereabouts. Again it goes back to choices, the choices that a father makes can severely wound his child, and that wound will be open well into their adulthood stage. I've interviewed many fathers, baby daddy's, ex-husbands on the matter of where the blame lies, and they accept some blame but not the entire blame because of the concerns already mentioned above. They'd say, "How can I be a father if she won't let me?" or "I tried staying for the kids, but it only got worse." and "All she wanted was the money." Although some may believe these are valid reasons for not coming around your exes. But it doesn't fly when it comes to the child. There may have a point to the difficulty they must feel when they have an ex withholding visitation, phone calls, and letters from their kids because of their lack of finances or problems they had within their relationship. It's not fair to the child. Child support is designed to support the child, so when men say they don't want to pay her, it makes no sense to withhold monies she needs to maintain the child's needs. They need to eat every day, not every so often as men may claim he pays or gives her money. Children need essentials things, like food, clothes, and shelter, notwithstanding care giving, doctor visits, school supplies, etc. I understand the logic behind withholding the child from contact with a father who isn't paying his child support, but I can't entirely agree with it. This tactic is damaging to the child and the relationship with their father. On the flip side, I understand men saying they only want to pay for the child's rearing and not to the mother's pampering. I disagree with this tactic as well, but I understand. Both tactics are damaging to the development of the children. The lack of funds for kids to do activities with their peers, mothers working more and spending less time home with her child can lead to the child grouping with the wrong crowd, crimes, introduction to drugs etc. Men not able to support and denied visitation of their child can lead children to the exact same outcome. So I see both sides and understand both arguments. It's a revolving cycle. She denies him access to their child because he doesn't pay, and he doesn't pay child support because he doesn't have access to his child. There are no winners in this game, but a clear loser, and that's the child. I had the chance to speak privately with a little girl from one of the single mothers I interviewed. I asked her, "Where is your father?" She replied, "I dunno, he didn't pay the child support." I was blown away by the mere fact she knew that, but I was more concerned about her real-life answer that she's attached her father to. This will undoubtedly affect her relationship with her father and carry on into her adulthood.

It can create a domino effect throughout her life. She could feel as if her father didn't think she was worth paying for, making her feel unworthy or worthless. That can lead to depression, anxiety, suicide, or being sexually provocative at a younger age. Which can possibly lead into a dating prostitution. With the mindset of making men pay for her. I'm not talking about men and women courting each other, I'm referring to those who think that if he pays he loves her and all she want is to be loved. Responsible fathers would spoil their little girls so that they wouldn't need a man for anything. He would honor her and display respect letting her know that she can ask him for anything. This builds a long lasting confidence in her and she now knows her worth isn't for sale, but a given.

I'm simply a provocateur of thought, giving my take on what I've researched, seen, heard, and lived through. By no means do I proclaim myself a professional in the fields of psychology or child development, but I did research in those fields and combined them with my eye test and life experiences dealing with children. I've been closely observing their growth and getting a better understanding of the fatherless development and functionality. What's the difference between a child with a father growing up and one who did not? Would they both grow up to be fine? Maybe, but their emotional toll and anguish would be the difference.

Fredrick Douglas said it best, "It is easier to build strong children than to repair broken men." There are some things synonymous between those that were raised with and without a father.

In some cases, the child raised without a father can feel as though they don't need a father to be successful and then prove it by figuring life out on their own. Then you have the child that had a father in the home, giving them guidance and reassurance along the way and their success resulted from example. Both came to successful conclusions. This most definitely can happen, but the ratio of this happening is heartbreakingly one-sided. The child with a father as an example will more likely succeed than one without. Listen, I get it. People date, marry, procreate, divorce, then date again, it happens. There is no reason to leave the little one you've created behind. Everyone agrees that the most crucial criterion in the family dynamics is the children and their emotional security. Protecting them from psychological damage and trauma should be pinnacle.

Being the Director of Youth Leadership Camps for over twenty years has taught me a lot about self. Our program took hundreds of kids from all over Los Angeles, San Bernardino, and Ventura County in California and gave them camping and social experiences that will last a lifetime. It's an excellent experience for children to meet other children from different areas and cultural backgrounds. Our camps focused on bettering our youth and giving them the tools to handle life away from the city streets. I recall one hot summer day on the campgrounds, and I had just finished up prepping my counselors on new protocols. The campers were all on free time where they're able to play board games, hike, swim, learn archery, play sports, do wall climbing, arts and crafts, or relax. I remember strolling through, debating with a pair of teens on religion and dating, sharing with them about what God says about being single and being married. The camp was bustling with kids enjoying themselves. Then I heard splashing from the lake followed by a billow of laughter. Someone must have fallen into the lake, which wasn't odd because kids fell in the lake all the time, and the bystanders would get a big kick out of it. So, I wasn't hurried to investigate, but the laughter quickly turned into campers yelling directions like, "Grab the paddle! Get back into the canoe!" My attention was immediately diverted towards the commotion and ended my debate and trotted off. Upon arrival at the lake's edge, it was just as I thought, one of the campers had fallen into the lake, and everybody was pointing and laughing. The camper was trying to get back into the canoe he fell out of, but the buoyancy kept it turning over like a rolling log.

All the surrounding kids were laughing and pointing. The other kids in canoes offered their assistance, but as he reached out for them, in his panic, he would accidentally flip their canoes over as well, which made the children laugh even more historically. There were three campers in the lake, but my focus was on the initial camper because he was the only one without a life jacket. He was one of my kids from the inner city, tough kid, gang-affiliated, no father in the home, and brought up by his grandmother. He was a big shot to his peers and a so-called playboy to the ladies. His reputation only added to the hilariousness of him falling into this dirty lake. I assume his reputation of being the hard cool kid was probably, why he didn't have his life jacket on in the first place.

Every summer, my counselors and I stress the importance of having life jackets on while canoeing in the lake, but the cool kids habitually break this rule. This particular camper was so cool that his pride wouldn't even allow him to yell for help, and that was the main reason why no one panicked or yelled out help for him. He camouflaged his panic and fear with a nervous smile as he reached out for the other canoes for safety. I immediately recognized that he couldn't swim. His nervous smile took to panic, and his dog paddling led to exhaustion. Seeing that camper flopping around in the lake flashed me back to when I was about his age and not knowing how to swim myself, but trying to be cool in front of my friends and acting as if I could. I mean, how hard can it be? I jumped right into the deep end of the pool, and couldn't touch the bottom. I panicked and took in some water, I was drowning, and no one knew it, because they were all jumping in themselves and splashing and having fun. All I could do was hold my breath and sink to the bottom of the pool and push back up to the surface to get air. I repeated that until I got so tired of sinking and coming back up for air that I then yelped for help. One of my friends noticed me and grabbed a cleaning pole and stretched it out to me, I grabbed hold it, and he pulled me to safety. In a nanosecond, that moment in my childhood immediately came to mind as I watched this inner-city kid expression turn from an embarrassing smile to an impetuous panic. Within seconds, I kicked off my boots and leaped right in. I swam over, grabbed him, and told him to calm down or else we would both drown. Although I can now swim, I've never rescued anyone before in my life, but what I did know was that a drowning person is desperate and will grab hold of whatever or whomever to stop drowning.

I couldn't allow him to grab me, so I swam around to his backside and grabbed him from around the neck. It was difficult and after a few peddles towards safety I began to lose momentum and felt myself tiring and sinking. Thank God I made it close enough to at least touch the muddy bottom and reach up and push him from underneath towards the embankment. I kept coming up for air and going back down, like when I was in my friend's pool drowning, he was flopping his arms trying to stay afloat on every shove I could give him. I did that at least five more times, and we finally reached enough shore to crawl out. He walked out, but I stayed plopped in the shallows, exhausted, catching my breath on my hands and knees. No applause, no thank you's, nothing but teenagers laughing at our ordeal and muddy wet clothes. He walked off, business as usual, back to being the cool guy that doesn't need any help. Wiping the mud off his clothes and threatening a beat down to all those who were laughing at him. This kid was so removed from displaying anemic emotions that he couldn't even yell for help. We cannot fault the youth for not exhibiting emotions other than anger when something moves them. When I counsel children that have difficulties displaying any other emotion besides anger I believe it comes from a couple of different sources, but one that stands out most is them having unresolved issues at home due to absent or invalid parents. So, I wasn't surprised that he didn't thank me or that his pride almost killed him because he didn't want to appear helpless. This kid inadvertently acquired independence way too early in his childhood and now refuses help from any outsiders in fear of being disappointed. Most fatherless children have built this immune to not having a father around and feel as though they don't need a father or anything that resembles one. Many teens and young adults are drowning, but will not verbally ask for help, even though their actions scream for it through their behaviors. It's a clear cry for help when someone hides their emotions. We, the lucky ones to have made it to adulthood, needed help at one time or another or else we would have drowned too. If it weren't for the lifeline of an attentive friend or caring relative, we could still be drowning. We should take time to save those who are acting out or drowning around us and not just negatively comment or take pictures and video of their drowning, but throw them a lifesaver.

This book is my lifesaver to those who feel as though they are still drowning and can't seem to catch their breath. Children who grew up not knowing their fathers felt abandoned and wouldn't ask for help because they were ignorant of the help they needed. In an analogy, on that drowning inner-city camper, the missing life jacket represented his absent father, and the canoe he fell out of was his mother. Once he left the safety of the canoe, his mothers care, he needed his life jacket, which was his father's wisdom. A mother can't keep their children afloat forever. They will eventually fall in deep waters, fall into the wrong crowd, fall into drugs or pre-marital sex, fall into depression, or at its worse fall into suicidal thoughts. A father can't keep children from falling, but with his presence he can keep them afloat.

The father is the life jacket.

Without the life jacket, children are susceptible to drowning. They can drown into depression, into anxiety, into gangs, into debt, jail, or in other word's they can drown in their environment's deepest waters. A drowning child remains blameless. Growing up in a fatherless home, they're just paddling around in a canoe looking for their life jacket.

EACH ONE TEACH ONE

We are teaching our children with our actions. Passive parents make passive kids; funny parents tend to have children that have a sense of humor. Aggressive fathers instill aggression in their sons, and emotional mothers usually pass those emotions on to their daughters. Because we're already living in a world with enough problems, monitoring our children should be paramount, because angry children can develop into angry adults. This isn't in all cases because there are children who recognize that their parents aren't infallible and they'll do a complete 180. They aren't aggressive, and they're not overly emotional. It's like two magnets, and both have an immense force to attract or repel. As we teach our children to love and respect others, we also have to teach them that others' feelings are just as important as their own. Children do not grasp why they feel the way they do; it becomes a confusing place to be in. It's our job, as adults, to recognize their confusion and explain those foreign feelings to them. Do you remember seeing your mother cry in a moment of happiness and wonder why? It confuses us as children, and we can only rely on the adults around us to explain it. As a child, when something angers or annoys us, we tend to feel and portray that same feeling outward. You hit me, I hit you, you pulled my hair, I kicked your shin. I see you play with a ball, and I want to play with the ball too. As we grow older, we understand more about how to control ourselves and not to be so reactionary. That's why it's important to monitor children, pre-teens, and even young adults when displaying disruptive behavior. It's essentially a subtle cry for help. Sometimes, it's the only way they know how to be heard and protect themselves from an even more painful emotion. Anger is used as a defense mechanism to hide an unmet need too painful to acknowledge. This can be long-lasting and repetitive as a person develops into an adult. Not having a father in the home for a significant portion of their childhood or absent entirely can leave an emptiness only a father can fill. Most don't even know why they're depressed, have anxiety, or easily angered. These are all psychological effects of growing up in a fatherless home, but it's that anger that manifests itself through the hurt and pain of feeling rejected by their fathers. They must then come to a place of managing their injuries and subsequent reactive responses; otherwise, it can lead to the unjustified outburst. Loved ones are the usual recipients of these outbursts.

Anger is sneaky, and a person may not even realize they're upset until they're upset. It affects the whole body. First, emotional, where suspicion sets in. Then, behavioral, which is the result of resentment, and finally cognitive where she/he believes the offender offended them purposely. When these things all align, a person can go from zero to a hundred real quick. The source of that anger comes from frustration and the threat of their emotions being exposed, and the powerlessness they have to it.

In many cases, it's that powerlessness that causes men to be violent. I don't condone violence, but for purposes of explanation, at least their anger reveals itself in some form of action. It's the children that don't outwardly express their outrage that worries me. Instead, they internalize it, feeling powerless in their own lives, causing them to displace that anger onto their parent, siblings, classmates, or even their pets. Both internal and external anger are signs of developing problems that must be met with direct attention and must not be ignored as assumed growing pains. Find out the root of what's going on with the child; welcome them to explore their feelings and concerns with you. This is key to a positive solution, and it gives a better understanding of the child to adult relationship.

Children living with anger can be an isolated space. They cause unnecessary tension in the safest of places and problems where problems don't exist. Most don't want to be around them, and others only deal with them out of fear. This creates bullies and artificial relationships early on. Feeling ostracized from others only feeds the anger more. Being easily angered causes constant combative discussions, potential rage, un-debatable debates, and ultimately violent confrontations. They don't mean to, it's just that they're hurt and in pain themselves, and as the saying goes, "Hurt people hurt people." If we as a village don't take control and respond to their obvious cries for help, their childhood years will be plagued with unnecessary conflict and even more pain.

Of course, my interpretation of an angry child or angry adult is built upon other corresponding components such as how they were parented, their environment, or social surroundings, and not solely on a fatherless home. Together, these things all contribute to a child carrying their anger into their adult life. So, I ask, where does that anger generate from so early on? Could it be from the feeling of abandonment or actual abandonment? Could that play some part in a person's character growing up? I believe so, always living with a chip on your shoulder and feeling like you have something to prove can be a lonely road to walk. Sometimes these people walk it alone, not allowing anyone in, and pushing everyone away. This way, they don't have to be accepted or be denied by anyone. Being denied acceptance, which is a very important human trait, can cause a snowball of effects in a person's behavior. It can cause them to be hesitant to meet new people out of fear of being denied. They then become experts on camouflaging their emotions. If they show that they don't care, then they won't be let down in the end. It makes it easier for them to display standoffishness and anger, but the longer this is carried on, the more it will define their identities as they grow further into adulthood. Why do abandon or perceived abandoned adults need anger management? And why don't those that need it refuse to believe they need it? I believe that when trauma happens to them, especially men, they don't think therapy is the remedy. They believe it's not natural for men to hug each other or even have a good cry. This is absolutely nonsense, both men and women that have anger issues believe that they're perfectly fine and it's everyone else that have problems and in need of treatment. As a result of this thinking, they come off as aggressive and rigid. There's lots of hurt and pain within them that they'll redistribute onto innocent bystanders if not addressed. Hurt people hurt people. Most of them are emotionally wounded people that bleed onto other people that didn't even cut them. They'll find themselves lashing out on people who didn't even deserve it, because of something that hurt them earlier in the day, earlier in the month or earlier in their childhood. That's not fair.

We all must take accountability for our actions. It's when we aren't ready to acknowledge our behavior when that accountability feels like an attack. We're walking around wounded, bleeding hearts that won't allow anyone to heal us out of fear of being hurt any further, attacking those that attempt to get to the bottom of our issues. To not allow someone to help you is simply outside of sanity, which is insanity. Of course, I'm being a bit facetious, although acting out of anger is a form of not being of sound mind. To be fair, everyone has had an episode of anger, but we don't consider ourselves to be mentally deranged. It's what we do in that moment of madness that deranges us.

I reached out to an old college classmate and practicing anger management counselor, Miss Danita, for her perspective on the correlation between anger and abandonment. She told me that not only does it correlate, but fatherlessness could very well be the key reason why some of her clients are angry in the first place. It all boils down to traumas in their childhood, and abandonment is likely the number one reason it severely affects them. Miss Danita and I were on the same page in our aspirations to bring awareness to the effects of fatherlessness on adults. Being abandoned, emotionally, or physically can and will leave a stain on a person's heart. We talked about it for hours. She even invited me to sit in on her sessions to observe some of those effects for myself. I couldn't pass up on this wonderful opportunity to witness and document how people come to be assigned anger management. Listening in on and interviewing her participants would be paramount for my research. So, I wasted no time in accepting her offer and showed up the very next day. I sat in on weeks of sessions and got to know her clients personally, interviewing some and crying with others. My findings were just as I expected, and those case studies ended up being the muse to my manuscript. I've read tons of books and sat through many lectures that dealt with the effects of abandonment. But to have the opportunity to witness the after-effects up close and personal was a total blessing.

She shared with me that most of her clients are referred to from the state and must go through the course to satisfy the courts. Although she doesn't solve anger issues but rather reveal the root of the issues that causes the anger, I thought would be a perfect addition to this book. Let's take a walk. When I was studying to be a Cognitive Behavioral Therapist, I learned that people weren't broken. Therefore, they didn't need fixing. They just needed to change the way they were thinking about themselves. I would help them avoid the untrue thoughts they had of themselves that their past has predicted and walk them through the readjustments necessary to begin anew.

Like my college colleague, we both would offer up management skills to our participants to better deal with their situation. My job is to get clients who see themselves as they are and not how they think others see them. That's a difficult enough task to accomplish without peeling back layers and layers of childhood pains. When I meet with people, my goal is to retrain that person's negative thinking and weaken their destructive behavioral patterns. I connect their childhood events to their current thoughts of themselves, which governs the emotions that eventually become their behaviors. The outcome of who they thought they were before our sessions aren't always who they are after. For example, I remember during one of my sessions, a young man told me that he was a thug, and I had to challenge him on that. "Who told you, you were a thug? Where did this begin?" He believed his environment and the people he associated with made him who he was, but it was none of those things. I first had to tell him who he was and who he was not. He was not who his friends said he was or his street address on which he lived on. I had to peel away all the preconceived thoughts of himself away before showing him who he really was. Shedding light on fatherlessness that continues to afflict our generation is an easy light to shine. The difficult part is finding those that want to unearth and unbury their stories. I'm hoping to find participants to draw a direct line from their childhood to adulthood through their fatherlessness.

I was eager to discover how positively or negatively it had impacted their lives. My hopes were high and rightfully so, in America approximately 15 million children live without a father in the home. Of that 15 million, 40% is of the Black and Latino communities. One could surmise that it's no wonder why there's anger amongst those communities. But this would be a falsity. There are many consequences to growing up without a father in the home, anger, or being angry because it is only one. Observing an anger management group, I wondered if they would open up to me about their fathers and how significant his presence was or was not to their lives.

Counselor Danita warned me that nine times out of ten, the people that attend her group therapy aren't readily open and upfront with their personal lives. It takes time to open them up.

She adds that it's a summation of their fears and their distrust of strangers and over time they've created habitual defenses to protect themselves from being hurt again. Those defenses have dug a groove into them like a heavy trekked dirt trail worn down and molded by a dirt bike's knobby tires. It has made them who they are, but not who they would otherwise be. All of us have personal defenses that protect us from pains, hurts, embarrassments, ridicule, etc. The problem is that those self-imposed defenses tend to take the lead and become us, and the longer we live behind the veil of them, the more we assume that to be our true identities, but it is not. You've heard before, in dating that when you meet a person for the first time, you're not really meeting them, you're meeting their representative. The person they want you to believe they are, but not who they really are, completely. Sometimes representatives are needed to get what you want from the relationship, and other times it backfires and causes even more damage than what it was meant to protect you from. It's out of fear that a person would hold back who they are before letting their guards down. It takes time to get to know someone and understand who they are, so consequently, getting to know someone in a dating relationship is no different than getting to know someone in a counselor-client relationship. It takes time to get to the core of who they are after peeling back the layers of who they want us to believe they are. Counselor Danita believes that stripping away those defensive layers and revealing past influences will allow me to extract the data needed to complete my task. It's not easy for people to be open and honest about something so personal and conceivably painful. My goal is to unearth those pains to help them release past pains so that they are able to function as the person they were meant to be.

Come inside a session with me. I was ultra-excited and wasted no time showing up bright and early the next morning with note pad in hand. The class was already in session. As I entered, I lowered my head and held my finger up as if I were excusing myself during church. She immediately introduced me to excuse my tardiness, "Everyone this is, Mr. Patrice Paul Garrett, he's a Cognitive Behavioral Therapist and will be observing our sessions for the next couple weeks." The class mumbled a couple of pleasantries as I sat down, and that was it. We were off. This setting was warm and comforting. She had scented candles lit and healthy green house plants surrounding a circle of couches and chairs in this small but well-lit office suite. One woman stood out immediately. Let share her story. She was a twenty-seven-year-old Latina woman, socially normal, but seemed to have a permanent disgusted look on her otherwise pretty face. Because her story deals with anger and aggression combinatory to abandonment, I'll identify her as ANGRY ANGIE. Throughout the chapters I'll use parallel nicknames that pertain to everyone's stories instead of using their real names.

Listening to Angie's back story, she tells us a string of stories of her being in and out of trouble as a teen as if it were a badge of honor. She shares that her father was very disrespectful to her mother and she kicked him out when she was eleven. He never returned. I believe this is the basis of her anger and self-imposed hatred due to the fact that her father abandoned the family during her pre-teens. So we have a foundation of the anger, let's find out what choices were made that led her to anger management.

Angry Angie paints a vivid picture of a date night gone wrong at a movie theatre last fall. She and a boyfriend got into a big fight, and both had to attend separate domestic violence and weeks of anger management classes. While sitting in the theatre waiting for the show to start, she recants her boyfriend's phone lighting up with a text. She glanced over and recognized it's an ex-girlfriend's phone number. He quickly tried to shield it from her sight, but it was too late.

She grabbed his phone and began to berate him with profane accusations. Voices were raised, and people started to notice, although the on-screen movie didn't start. The off-screen drama surely had people eating their popcorn waiting to see wait was next. She stood over him, slapping his face and cursing him out. She says he tried to explain, but all she saw was red. She was furious. He stood up and grabbed her wrist and tried taking his phone back, but she snatched away from him and shuffled down the isle and ran out of the theatre. He gave chase through the lobby and into the women's restroom. As you can imagine, movie management had no choice but to intervene and call the police. Statements were given, and needless to say, they both got charged for domestic aggravation in a domestic dispute. It was her second offense. She tells the group that she initiated a fight with a girl who disrespected her in high school. Such as in this current story, disrespect is her obvious trigger. She believed that he was being disrespectful and she was taught not to tolerate a man's disrespect. Her beliefs led to thoughts, and her thoughts to feelings to which ended ultimately with her actions. This isolated event told me a lot about what she thought of herself. Reacting in the manner she does is a overreaction to the violations that were set forth. For numbers on a cellular device to have the power to enrage a person comes from a deeper place. I believe that her level of anger and reactivity is related to her childhood pain and the disrespect she witnessed her mother go through with her father. It'll first take her to recognize her triggers in order to manage her emotions better and begin the healing process. Aligning her childhood experiences to her actions as an adult is where the first layer of peeling begins.

COUNSELOR - Let's set your boyfriend's actions aside momentarily and talk about your actions and what you could have done to deescalate the situation.

ANGRY ANGIE - Nada! Because I didn't do anything to deserve that from him. I'm tired of guys treating me like shit. If he thinks he can get away with doing that in my face, I'm gone kick his ass.

The group chuckles.

COUNSELOR - Did you witness abuse between your parents while growing up?

ANGRY ANGIE - My father, if you can call him that. He was always disrespectful to my mother, smacking her around and talking down to her. My brothers would get in the middle of it, but I would stay in my room. I could hear them fighting all the time.

COUNSELOR - What did your mother do in response to the disrespect?

ANGRY ANGIE - She took it until he started threatening us. Pushing my brothers around and cursing at me. Then she finally stood up for herself. One day he came home drunk, yelling and cursing at everybody because the empty trash bin wasn't taken in from the street. He was being disrespectful and embarrassing her. So later when he went to sleep that night, she threw a hot pot of menudo on him and beat him with the pan. (She laughs) He left a week later. (Her laugh slows to a breathy chuckle) He never came back.

COUNSELOR - Did that upset you? That your father never came back? Do you blame your her?

ANGRY ANGIE - No. It was his fault. He pushed her to do it. What was she supposed to do, let her kids get abused like her? I blame him. She had no choice.

COUNSELOR - She had a choice, so did he. Everyone has a choice, Angie. A person's pre-decision predicts the pressure of the choices they'll eventually have to make, but it's our choice and our actions behind those choices that were made. Do you think you had the option of choosing to walk out of the theatre that day when you felt disrespected by your boyfriend?

ANGRY ANGIE - Not really, he was my ride. (she laughs)

COUNSELOR - Angie.

ANGRY ANGIE - I could have, but I didn't. People force me to react. So I do. They must want it, so I give them what they want.

Blame shifting and deflection are normal responses for Angry Angie when it comes to accepting responsibility for her actions. She believes that if she is willfully provoked, then the repercussions that follow are justified. Her actions are reactions to what someone else has done to her; therefore, they got what they deserved. Angie's childhood experiences have taught her that she can use anger to control others (like her father) or be controlled (like her mother). Her issues with the boyfriend are much bigger than him cheating. In retrospect, we could replace him with anyone, like a disrespectful boss, someone cutting her off in traffic, or a girlfriend abandoning her at a bar to hook up with some random guy. The outcome will be the same because any signs of disrespect or abandoning take her back through that emotional injury she experienced in her childhood. When her father unexpectedly left the family, that wounded her and left an emptiness that she never forgave him for. When her emotional injuries weren't addressed or resolved as a youth, she found anger to be the more comfortable feeling to display than dealing with her feelings of being hurt or disappointed. Because Angie has been ignoring and blocking those unwanted emotions, the slightest of offenses would produce an aggressive outburst. Generally, over time repressing painful feelings would only compound upon itself and yield hate and resentment, which only further fuels the anger at its outburst.

There's no doubt that relationships are hard, and infidelities are the usual suspects for ending them. However, people who have emotional injuries from troubled childhoods should first identify those repressed pains and the idiosyncrasies attached to those pains in order to succeed in healthy relationships. How can we expect someone else to understand us if we don't understand ourselves? There's a little bit of Angry Angie in all of us, but our preceding actions make the difference and separate us. In our sessions, I've noticed that Angie would constantly shift blame onto others, "People force me to react." she says in one of her many statements. Though a reaction is a counter to some sort of action. Words, or opinions against a person, is not a physical action. Therefore, that person's initial physical action would be the cause of that aggression. Anger always has other emotions that precede it, such as fear, shame, guilt, jealously, embarrassment, or perceived disrespect in Angie's case. Angie would attach whatever she thought was disrespectful to any violator and validate her outburst. Right or wrong, she felt justified, which would further suppress what she was feeling deeper inside. This "disrespect" trigger was created in her by witnessing her mother being disrespected by her father, so lashing out in aggression was in fact a normal response to any disrespectful offense for her. I want to be clear; Angie being disrespected is not okay, and someone not respecting her or her boundaries is not okay. The problem exists when she perceives everything that threatens her repressed emotions as disrespect and then rationalizes her aggression instead of facing her true feelings. Using a rationalization form of defense make it to never be her fault as to why she's angry. It's always someone else's. Fatherless children/adults dealing with anger issues usually abuse other people to feel some sort of relief for the hurt and pain they feel within themselves.

Like most fatherless adults, they're oblivious to the origin of that anger or even realize that they're the actual transgressor in their volatile situations. Anger is only their mask to other suppressed emotions. We need to show the Angry Angie's of the world that anger is a feeling like any other feeling; it's okay to feel angry or upset. It's what you do with that anger that separates the civil and the severe, the normal and the abnormal. Easily angered people should find constructive ways to release their anger. Find intensive physical activities like cross-training, boxing, martial arts, or intermediate sports where those aggressive emotions can be released. Ignoring them or bottling them up isn't healthy at all. It's only a matter of time before something triggers those emotions that'll cause the next outburst. Waiting to solve those issues during an outburst is like trying to stop a stick of dynamite from exploding once the fuse has already been lit. Their struggles with undesirable feelings and emotions can cause levels of stress, anxiety, and depression that can lead them to self-medicate. i.e., opioids, marijuana, or cocaine. What's worse than ignoring unwanted emotions and anxieties is trying to medicate them away with drugs. If diagnosed and properly prescribed by a physician, it's okay, but it'll be a good choice to steer clear of recreational drugs while figuring out your life. Any drugs, prescribed or otherwise while dealing with suppressed emotions, do one of two things, either heighten the sensitivity of your triggers, or gives a crutch to your already bad behavior. When it comes to sorting out your childhood pains and unwanted emotions, it's best to have a clear mind that's not clouded by anything that will blur the lines of your truth.

When it comes to relationships associated with repressed emotions, a repeatedly damaged person will begin shopping for what they need and no longer for what they want. The need for security and safety will overshadow their wanted desires of aesthetics and status. This, in itself, can be problematic without first doing the work in finding out why their wants were more important than their needs in the first place. A person can take on and become their frequently used defense mechanism, but it's not who they really are. They've just adapted to something that they were using to protect themselves. A boxer isn't always boxing, their learned defenses is only of use when in the ring not in the office. A damaged person who hasn't sought out the origin of their hurt will manufacture and disguise their wants. They will then choose a partner, and before long, they begin to hate those disguised parts of their partner and then blame them for not being those things they initially wanted. That person's decisions were solely based on who they thought they were and what they felt needed. That leads to poor decision making. Remember, with growth; you'll evolve into a different person with a different set of criteria for what you're looking for in a partner. Summarily, once a person figures out the source of their pain, their needs will change as they have.

Many different things can activate triggers, a picture, a place, a song, a person, an event, a thought, or a word. My advice to all the Angry Angie's is to recognize the source of your triggers. Do not suppress the emotions connected to them, or else it can end in an implosion of anger and aggression. Secondly, avoid toxic relationships. Call out those red flags early on in a relationship and note them as an intuitive warning to your heart. Lastly, always seek self-improvement. Don't be satisfied with living with emotional pain and then become complacent with being your defense mechanism. Move forward to a better you. Franklin D. Roosevelt states it best, "There are many ways of going forward, but only one way of standing still." Don't stand in the past of your childhood; move forward.

Single AND a Mom

Sitting in on these sessions, I saw that the participants were learning from each other's' experiences and the feedback that followed. They vowed to apply it to their situations. The day I spoke with BABY MOMA MONIQUE, a black woman in her early 30's, I was impressed with the wisdom she had and the feedback she gave. She was very opinionated and chimed in on practically everything asked of the other participants. On numerous occasions, before the group would begin, I would catch everybody intensely listening to her sharing gems on cooking recipes, fashion tips, children, and practically had an opinion on an array of subjects. She's a single parent of two boys by two different fathers. At the time, her teenager was in jail, and her other child was still a toddler. She said she'd tried everything to keep the streets from eating her kids up, i.e., going to jail or joining a gang. She signed them up in every after-school program to give her time to get home from work to pick them up from school. She allows her mother to keep them most of the time. Baby Moma Monique complains that the neighborhood she lives in lacks good role models and feels like they are always trapped inside the house. She says she's afraid to let them play with the other kids outside, but her teenager does what he wants. She agrees that her choice of men she dates has been terrible. Monique was in jeopardy of losing them both to foster care unless she completed these court-ordered sessions. She tells this story in full detail, unapologetic with no punches pulled. She confides that the guy she was dating and subsequently had her youngest child with, turns out to be a drug dealer, selling marijuana out of lawn mower repair shop she believed him to have. Unlike in some states today, marijuana was illegal to sell, purchase, grow, or consume back then. Sadly, Baby Moma Monique and the father of her son, or the more popular term, the baby daddy, house that they shared was raided for drugs, and in the process, her kids were taken away by Child Protective Services. He went to jail for his third strike, and in California, the law mandates if a person gets three felony convictions, three strikes, that person is to be sentenced to no less than 25 years of life imprisonment. She was left to financially fend for herself, foundationally raise two boys into becoming men, and repair her broken relationship. The ladder, being the least important of the three, but critically important for her sons.

Listening to Baby Moma Monique tell her story, I wondered how the little girl Monique became the adult Monique? What roads did she travel to get to the destination of who she was today? And what role did her father play in her life? Through her sharing in the group, I learned that her immediate problems with CPS were the only thing she wanted to discuss in the group, nothing else. From my observation, I can conclude that Monique's been dealing with some deep-seated pain. It was a clear sign of anxiety and depression. Counselor Danita was tapping in on a sensitive subject for Monique. Her kids. Talking about her children only made Monique more elaborate with her body language and more passionate in her speech. The fact that she has to go through this process of paying for and being a part of therapy got her annoyed. But I suppose that's what therapy is all about. It's like an orange; you must peel off the outer layer to reveal the individual slices inside of it. I'm interested in the juicy slice that deals with her father.

Counselor Danita usually would give 15-minute smoke breaks, and those are the times I would take advantage of the opportunity to have one-on-one interviews with group members. During our break today, I followed Monique down the hall to the restrooms to inquire more about her life. She needed someone to align with her and be empathetic to her situation, so I drummed up a CPS conversation and how it was overdue for some vast improvements. She agreed, then I told her how blessed I was to have had my mother's strength when my father was absent. The peeling was gone, and I plucked a nice juicy slice because she eagerly told me that she never knew her father. She added that the little information she did have from her mother was that her father moved to Louisiana shortly after she was born, and they never had any more contact. Monique says the times her mother did mention him. It was always in an undesirable light. So, she felt ashamed to show any interest in a man her mother despises. She grew up resenting a father she never knew and giving him power over her emotions.

She further explains that it's people who are the problem, and it's the world that needs rehabilitating, not her. The fact that as an adult, she believes nothing is wrong with her, and the problem lies with others, made her a prime candidate for this course and a perfect subject for my book.

When we came back from break, Counselor Danita wasted no time in evaluating Monique,

COUNSELOR - Why do you think you choose the type of men that aren't necessarily good for you or your children?

MONIQUE - They choose me, but at one time, I did think who would want me anyway? I would go with those type of men because I didn't have many choices. Besides at least they made money. They had potential, my last guy's father was doing life in prison. So his grandmother raised him, but she was too old to keep up with him and what he was into. So, he started slanging weed here and there, just to friends and people in the neighborhood, then I began to see strange people stop by his grandmother's house. So, since we were dating, I let him move in with me. He paid all the rent and took care of my son. We made it work, then I got pregnant with his son, around that same time crack cocaine was the new thing. He started dealing with that, and that's when all hell broke loose. He was a product of his environment, and so was I.

Monique, a single mother, not having a father in the home herself growing up, is on a constant search for a father replacement: a dominant figure, someone who can protect them. It's not a surprise that in impoverished communities women prefer to date bad boys or thugs because it makes them feel safe. Single mothers that grew up fatherless tend to choose men that they believe will be good fathers. A strong father figure, something she never had growing up. A man that she wished her father could have been.

COUNSELOR - The men you are choosing to father your children are children themselves. They're emotionally undeveloped. They're making poor decisions and taking an unnecessary risk, are clear signs of immaturity. Just like you need them to be a loving, caring father and mate, they need you to make up for the empty, lonely parts of their childhood. Do you think that your father affected you in some way for you to keep choosing the same type of men?

MONIQUE - Probably, I don't think about him. F*ck him. I do what I gotta do for my kids. My father wasn't around, and my mother made the best out of what she had! And so will I. I don't choose men that I think won't be there. How am I supposed to know they're assholes?

Monique's personal story is similar to many stories of single mothers who chose men that don't demonstrate a sense of family or personal responsibility. She was brought up with no father in the home, imprisoned or otherwise, and now her children are being raised the same way. It's a repeating cycle of irresponsible fathers. The story's the same; the only thing that changed was the names. This exchange with the Counselor was priceless. Although Monique says she doesn't think about her father or how he abandoned her, she subconsciously thinks about him all the time. Whether she knows it or not, it's apparent in the men she chooses, and yes, she chooses them regardless of her words that they choose her. That's her way of feeling validated. It's validation that she's worth being loved and has value to someone other than herself and her kids. It's crucial to her survival. These validation issues arise because her father wasn't in her life as a child. Unannounced to the pain of her abandonment has her feeling unworthy and unwanted in her adulthood. Statements like "Who wants me?" and "F*ck him" are clear signs of some deep-seated pain that she's been ignoring her whole life. She rationalizes to herself that the best way for her to deal with it was not to deal with it. She has disdain for her father, a stranger, someone she never knew. His absence will continue to disable her until she comes to grips with it. She says she has no choice, thinking she has to take what's given because she just thinks of herself as unworthy, unwanted, and discarded. Until she changes the way she thinks about herself, she will continue to make poor decisions in men. This isn't uncommon for women to choose poorly because of their upbringing. They either want to choose a guy like their father or a man totally opposite of him, whether she likes it or not. Men choose partners in the same way; they try to emulate and be just like their fathers or try hard to be nothing like him. Women will compromise their choices of men for security, and men will compromise their choice in women for status, but nonetheless, their choices will be based upon their fathers' influence and how they behave within a relationship, what they would or would not accept based on their upbringing and how they think about themselves. Women tend to internalize emotions, while men externalize theirs. In Monique's case, she's internalized her feelings for so long that she normalized self-hate and lacked self-worth. She doesn't even realize that she's doing it. She's one of millions that unknowingly do this to themselves, and we as adults will harbor things from our past and dock them into our present, but we need to recognize the hole in our vessel and patch it up before we sink deep into the abyss of mental illness. Monique and her kids' fathers all come from highly dysfunctional families that can and will cause mental illness. From there, the way one thinks of his/herself will reflect on how they move forward in life.

Being a single mother of two young boys is not so easy. The statistics are stacked against them. The U.S. Department of Health and Justice states that 63% of fatherless children from single-parent homes commit suicide, 71% drop out of high school, and 70% are in prison.

Of course, other disparities come into play, such as economics, education, and the environment. Still, when it's broken down to its core value, and we compare single-parent homes to both parents living in the house, there is a drastic difference in the children's behavior. This issue transcends class because there are many challenges facing mothers as they attempt to rear their male children. By nature, women take on the nurturing role and teach their male children the acceptance of vulnerability. When there's no father in a young man's life, it makes it easy to manipulate their mother's emotions, and as a result, there will be destructive activities they will be tempted to engage in. Young boys have this built-in masculine energy that needs to be fed, and without a way to channel it, they can become frustrated and fall into a destructive state. It's at those times where they make some of the worse impulsive decisions of their lives. A father's presence would show them how to manage that built up energy, and guide them through those impulses. Mothers can't teach their sons how to be men, just like single fathers can't teach their little girls how to be women. It's a balance that needs to be equally weighed by both ends of the scale.

I think it's imperative that we understand single mothers' pain, concerns, and anguish that they have to experience as they attempt to raise their sons and prepare them for the world. I've comprised a list of 10 DO's & DON'T's for single mothers when raising young boys:

1) DO allow your sons to have male role models. Without it, they won't respect masculinity, and in turn, won't respect women.

2) DON'T allow your son to EXPLOIT your tenderness. Let them fall and brush themselves off. Let them work out problems on their own. Mothers don't be too quick to assist and rescue them. Instead encourage them to find their own way with close supervision. Remember, the more you help, the more he'll exploit you, making him what his friends will call a Moma's Boy.

3) DON'T emasculate him. At a young age let him be rambunctious, run around, be dangerous and out of control sometimes.

4) DO encourage manhood by not making him adopt female values. Teach him to recognize female values, but not to adopt them. Allow his testosterone to grow. The male ego is different from the females. For example: in most cases, teasing a boy will end up in a fight. That's his masculinity being threatened so ego pops in. Teasing little girls, may result in a breakdown of crying where ego isn't the factor, but her self-esteem is bruised. Prepare your son for the day when he's around other boys, and he has his

Rights Of Passage. You don't want him to break down and cry, but to stand up for himself, whether verbally or physically. Men are territorial, let him be that.

5) DON'T feminize your sons. Draw a line in the sand. Boys are boys, and girls are girls. Little girls will gracefully develop, while little boys need to be built.

6) DO point out good men to him, then encourage him to emulate the positive traits in those men.

8) DON'T allow your personal views of men to destroy the young man you're raising.

9) DO treat men like you want others to treat your son. He's constantly watching.

8) DON'T title your son "The man of the house." Allow him to earn his way to be a man.

9) DO date, but don't introduce random guys to your sons. They're paying attention and can cause him to view women as sex objects.

10) DON'T demonize his father. Remember he is a reflection of him and will internalize those words for himself. You'll only be hurting your son when you speak badly of his father..

Make no mistake about it; single mothers are the ultimate blessing to a child's life. In my opinion, there's no replacement for a mother other than God Himself. My list of do's and don't's aren't to tell women how to raise their sons, it's only a help-aid from a son's point of view. If the mother constantly emasculates and demeans the boy's father, it can weaken the bond between he and the boy and damage his self-esteem. In most cases, the opinion he holds of his father is the same opinion he has of himself. If I can get single mothers to focus less on what they dislike about their sons' absent father, and instead concentrate more on their father's positive attributes they want their son to emulate, my job is complete. To add, always affirm your sons in their successes and encourage them to try again in their failures. Their fathers quit on them, and they need to understand that the "quitting" part is the failure, not them. Finally, while encouraging your sons, try not to" baby" them to the point of retarding their independence. Find a balance of softness and freedom that they can thrive in.

You can always spot a man raised by his mother. They're usually hypersensitive to criticism, petty, unreasonable, and have unbridled tempers. This is not to say they're maladjusted adults; single mothers raised some of our greatest men and leaders. But abandoned men brought up by a mother, grandmother, sister, or aunt are continually searching for their fathers' love, acceptance, validity, and approval. At times that's the driving force behind their success, but it is a fact that children raised in a two-parent household are twice as likely to succeed academically, financially, and socially. In this case, children who grow up without a father would attempt to complete a task, and as soon as it gets complicated, they would quit. Sons with fathers in the home would be encouraged to keep going until the task is complete or, at the very least, try again. Involved fathers won't allow mommy to come in and save the day or complete the task for them. We hear it all the time, "He's so spoiled." But why is that? It's because he gets what he wants when he pleads to his mother's emotions. The mother spoils him because she never wants to see him sad, hurt, or discouraged. It's in a woman's nature to nurture and coddle him. Single mothers need to understand that it's inevitable to prevent hurt and pains from happening to their sons. It's almost crucial that they experience some difficulties as a rite of passage, which grooms them for their future independence. So the sons that grow up emotionally shielded by their single mothers aren't equipped to deal with disappointments or failures because they will always seek out their mother's approval before making any decisions of their own. Making them dependant. Depending on their mother to make all the hard decisions in their lives. Even in their adulthood they would allow their mothers to dictate how their relationships should go. I'm not referring to simple mother/son advice, but outright followed demands. These children are usually referred to as "Moma's Boys." Moma Boys tend to be needier and have low expectations of their wives, girlfriends, or lovers because their mate can never measure up to their mother. Simultaneously, on the other end of the spectrum, researchers have reported that they can also become surrogate spouses, imitating their missing fathers' roles and duties in the home. When male children feel like they're filling the shoes of an absent father, it can confuse them on who they are. The son or the husband? This too can significantly impact her sons' adult life. He would parallel some of the same task in his mother/son relationship to his romantic relationships. This can give him confusing concerns with intimacy, and lead to questioning of his own sexual identification.

Son's relationships with their mothers shape their social, emotional, and cognitive development, but don't allow your sons to play grown-up while acting like irresponsible children, giving them the wrong impression of what men do. This distorts their independence. This false feeling of independency compels them into being disrespectful, unruly, or like mentioned before, spoiled. Spoiling children is a contributing factor of entitlement. Entitled children, sons, in this case, need to understand that things aren't just given to them out of duty but out of love. Their independence is to be earned through trust and responsibility. Can I trust you? Are you responsible? Giving a male child the title "Man of the House" does a disservice to him when it's not earned. I implore mothers to stay consistent without skipping steps, give sons a little tough love to allow them to grow naturally into the man you're raising. On the other end of the single mother spectrum is the son watching his Super Woman of a mother, doing it all. Providing, protecting, and disciplining. She may even say it aloud that she's his mother and his father. She had to be; she had no other choice. If something needs to get done, she will do it. She has no help-mate present to take on the duties of a missing man. She's so independently strong that when it's time for that young man to leave the nest and become his own man, he can't. He's so accustomed to mommy doing everything for him that he lacks the proper tools to do for himself. When other men, i.e., teachers, police officers, counselors, coaches, etc. try to step in; he has a hard time accepting their instruction. He never had to listen to a man tell him what to do before, so he resists; remember he was the "Man of the House". So, he rebels and challenges male authority and ritualistically screams, "You're not my father! You don't tell me what to do!". Can you blame them? Why should they trust and put their hope into strangers when they can't even trust their own fathers? Fatherless boys that resent their biological fathers will battle against other men attempting to give them guidance. They believe that if they don't allow themselves to love or trust another male figure, they can't be hurt by one.

In theory, taking power away from the male figure protects them from lingering pain that accompanies abandonment. But in principle it only gives them more power and more control over their emotions because they believe every man is like their father.

The fear of a reoccurring abandonment is what keeps that hole in a fatherless child's heart vacant and disqualifies any other man that tries to fill it.

Mothers seem to do a much better job preparing their daughters to leave the nest than their sons, and fathers seem to do a much better job preparing their sons than their daughters. It's only obvious that children mimic what they see in their parents, the hurtful and the helpful traits. If daddy shows independence, then his son will try to do the same, tie his shoes, pour his milk, and feed himself. If mommy displays a caring nature to others, her daughter will do the same, like caring for classmates in daycare or tending to their friend's injuries.

Single mothers don't set out to be single mothers. Who would sign up for that? And why is there a gradually rising rate of single-parent households? In the urban communities, in attempts to help disenfranchised families, the system actually assist in bringing it down. Society gives single women recourses like WIC (Women Infant Children) to subsidize their expenses without a man's financial support. If there's a man bringing income into the home, then the funding is terminated. So single mothers with government assistance aren't too quick to engage with their deadbeat dads if it means it will jeopardize their welfare check. This is counterproductive to grounding a stable family infrastructure in an already fragmented community. Single parent homes become even more fragmented when the courts step in.

Women are appointed lawyers by the family court system, while the men fight for their rights as fathers. They criminalize the men with alimony judgments, child support, and jail, furthering the separation and the possibility of a family reconciliation. The courts determine whether he's fit or she's stable, whether the kids live here or the kids live there, who gets time and who doesn't, and who pays money and who receives money. The courts have all the authority to rule over our family lives. Most of the time, men lose custody of their children to the mothers, which keeps the father away from the child more than bringing him closer. When the system takes the custody away from the fathers, the government becomes that child's daddy, and the mothers are in holy matrimony with the system.

I wonder if I can deconstruct the average single mother. Where does it start? Dating? The men and women that are destined to be single parents are the ones that begin with choosing partners using superficial criteria rather than their true bonding intuition. Men shouldn't date, sleep with, or procreate with women solely based on outer appearance. Looks change. Women shouldn't date, sleep with or procreate with their fantasies, believing that it will materialize in the relationship. Both men and women have dating expectations, but are sadly disappointed when these expectations don't come to fruition. Some would say they settled; some would say they thought he/she would change, but those red flags that were overlooked in the beginning because of their outer shell, career, status, or money is only the fault of the chooser. Ignoring signs of unequally yoked coupling have led many into a single parent lifestyle today. There are a myriad of other reasons and special circumstances that can severely damage couple bonds, but once they have children together, that bond is eternal. Therefore, there should be a different and deeper set of criteria judging that relationship, similar to solidifying a beaming romance with marriage vows. Promises and agreements are made in the mist of love and should be upheld, especially where the fate of their children's emotional future is at stake. People aren't thinking of a mate, but the act of mating.

They've commoditized children by choosing partners like they're choosing designer pets. He's tall; she has green eyes, he's dark, she has Italian blood. No one is taking having children seriously, or the importance of having both parents in the household and not just a sperm donor sending checks every month.

Statistics from the First Things First Foundation states that in the U.S. alone, 60% of all births are to single mothers. Couples are serious about having children, but not serious about each other. The statistics are disproportionately higher at an alarming 86% in

Black communities. That's an awful lot of children starting with parents that may not stay together. My contention is to popularize couples interfacing before marriage so that it'll cut down on unequally yoked coupling from the start. When you understand a person's values, morals, goals, theories, disciplines, and beliefs, it drastically changes a person's desire to or not to procreate. When these things are woven together it gives a more in-depth form of dating, not just dinner and a movie. People really need to get to know each other before the sheets get drawn. Asking a bunch of superficial getting-to-know-you questions isn't enough. You have to observe a person's character and their choices in several different situations before deciding to make an eternal bond with that person. Any short cuts to this, can and in most cases, will result in a break-up. Which isn't all bad, because it can be a learned experience to which each party finds their own personal development. A break up can educate an individual on what's tolerable and what is not, what they thought they could deal with, and what they could not. But when children are involved, things get more complicated. Now the decisions made will affect the children and their emotional, physical, and psychological state. There are no guarantees or magic wands that can make couples stay together after bringing life into the world. Still, we must take personal responsibility for dotting all the "I's and crossing all the T's" before conception, which translates to; Question every red flag and allow an efficient amount of time to observe a person's character. This may take a few seasons. Find your measuring stick of tolerance, and have it in mind that the little things you tolerate now will be your breaking point in the future.

Single parenting has been carried on from generation to generation. "My mother raised me on her own, and I can raise my children without a man as well." Women's empowerment has somehow gotten convoluted with women's independence. Being independent of a man is a woman's choice, and empowering oneself is a human choice.

See, what I've ascertained from dating and dating my race, in particular. Daughters of single mothers from the Baby Boomer era raised stronger black women, but weaker black men. By default, they've raised their daughters to take on the masculine role in relationships, by constantly telling them to be strong and independent, and that they don't need a man. Though the message is edifying, its slightly distorted because their mothers had to be strong and independent out of survival, not as a trendy catch phrase or slogan. On its surface this advice is protective, but what's being imbedded into their daughters is a defense mechanism designed to counter weak men. Some of which, were men that were raised by that same single mother with no male influences around.

Inevitably this generation was on a collision course for power from the start. It's a set-up to a future of failing relationships. Now don't get me wrong, I want our women to feel strong, safe and protected but quite a few single black mothers are raising their daughters to be single black mothers. Quick to leave the father of their children, because of the power struggle in the relationship.

The problem is that those single mothers spent more time on preparing their daughters to defend against boys pretending to be men, but not enough time on the recognition of what to do with a qualified good man. By the time their daughters go out into the dating world they aren't equipped with the ability to identify the wants and needs of wholesome men. So when these strong women come across strong men, they butt heads. It doesn't work. They're both, single parent bound. She then makes an emotional choice and begin to attract men that are needy, submissive, or looking for a mother and because she's used to being in charge and dominant, it feels familiar. After a while, it becomes tiring to always tell her man what to do and how to do it. She naturally wants to be feminine, protected and taking care of.

But of course he doesn't possess the ability to be that person because he lacks the tools himself. He too was raised by a strong, independent single mother and was dependant on a woman to tell him what to do. So he can't lead her. He can't step into the role she needs because he lacks the tools from his father. Now, when these two people have a child, they wonder why it doesn't work.

Individually, they need to be receptive to a qualified person, preferably a therapist, advising them, because they lack those identifiers of what's needed to relate with a partners and not just a lover.

When it comes to raising children and children's overall emotional health, men and women need each other. Can women raise children on their own? Yes. Should they do it alone? Absolutely not, and here's a list of reasons why:

1. Single mothers usually have a hard time balancing work and child-rearing, which puts them in financial strains.

2. Drug and or Alcohol abuse in adolescents is 75% higher from absent father homes.

3. Affects children's emotional health with depression, anxiety, and feelings of abandonment.

4. Education can suffer. 71% dropout rate.

5. Children from single-parent households have a higher chance of being involved in criminal activity and delinquent behavior.

6. Sexual activity, which raises the risk of teen to pre-teen pregnancy.

7. Suicide and suicide attempts are higher.

8. 80% of molesters and rapists come from an absent father home.

9. 90% of single parented household's have children that run away from home.

When I counsel young women that have children with who they deem questionable baby fathers, I share with them this list and encourage them to keep the father of their children active in their child's lives. Some reluctantly take the advice while others do not, claiming they don't need him, and their children would be better off without him. This type of woman has been bread to believe and react this way over time. They watched a deadbeat father abandon them, and a struggling mother do it alone, so they're conditioned in the same way. The slightest sign of the baby daddy not lining up with their expectations of what a father, boyfriend, or husband should be, they leave the relationship. These types of women have bought into the fact that they can leave if they're not happy. Images on social media and secretly unsupportive friends have given them the fortitude to throw away her family for what she presumes is happiness. They believe that they're being independent and strong, but they're being ignorant and wrong. The child's mental and emotional health is more important than their personal agenda against that man. You may not need your man, but your child needs his father. There are no trophies or badges of honor given to women that raise children on their own. Most will tell you it's a hard and harrowing road that they wished they didn't have to travel alone.

There's no I in dependence because children depend on both parents to raise them. It's okay to be empowered. It's something I encourage everyone to seek, but please don't confuse empowerment with independence. Women's independence is an empty term. Women have come a long way to feel equal to men because, in the past, women took on the vulnerable nurturing role, and men were expected to take on the competitive side of life. Balancing a family and a career was shunned upon in corporate America for women. That's why over the past two decades, media have been righting that wrong by showing us images of strong women, corporate women, heroine women in movies, and video games. We know women are amazing, and single women with children are Super Women, but we also know now the great importance and long-term benefits of a father's close involvement in a child's life. Let's not take away a child's right to know and bond with their biological father because a relationship between the two consenting adults didn't work.

I don't believe in punishing the son for the sins of his father. If she's not happy in the relationship, she has the right to leave the relationship, but there will be a lot of necessary adjustments to be made to ensure the child has a relationship with his/her father. Passion, anger, and general conflict are synonymous with relationships. Women react more when they feel betrayed, and men react more when they feel humiliated. Relationships are reactionary. Depending on the offense and the action after the reaction, measures the recovery of their connection. Some relationships die a slow death, and others live on to that happily ever after. If their union comes to an end, the baby conceived within it shouldn't be thrown out with the dirty bathwater. Getting a baby daddy doesn't guarantee he will be a daddy to that baby. People who have been previously hurt in relationships usually choose their next lover based on what their last lover lacked. That's not growth, that's routine. Instead of finding out more about oneself, they immediately go out to replace what was missing in their last relationship. Love can't live within those parameters. Those four walls of hurt, distrust, fear, and repetition, love will suffocate. They get hurt, stop trusting and then carry that fear into the next relationship. Hurt people searching for relationships usually withhold their feelings of love out of fear of being hurt again. This takes a much longer time for both parties to evaluate a person's true intentions and makes it more difficult to watch the seasons of that person's character. Then, before you know it, an unplanned pregnancy happens, and you're picking out baby cribs, pampers, and car seats.

When people date, they don't spend enough time considering that this great partner could be a horrible parent. Sometimes the signs are there. Suppose you're dating someone who already has kids but never mentions them or their parenting arrangement they have set up between the two, that should be a red flag. Please don't ignore it, question it. Women date what they need, and men date what they want. She needs security, and he wants loyalty, or she wants validation, and he wants sex. People date for a merit of different reasons, and most times, the engaging parties like each other in hopes to one day love each other. Suppose dating hasn't matured into a relationship by the time a child binds them together. In that case, that's a recipe for disaster, and they're one ingredient away from the single parent lifestyle. Whether it's by failed expectations, assumed assumptions, broken promises, misunderstandings, disagreements, or plain-old relationship immaturity. If the relationship is still in the evaluation stages. It could be in jeopardy of separation even before parenting begins, and more likely, the child is to be left with one parent. The single mom.

Dating and having a baby with someone you don't really know is like a couple taking a vacation; they have a good time, party it up, and make memories. While on that vacation. They purchase a plant as a souvenir to share in remembrance of their wonderful time together. When they get home, they show this cool plant to all their friends and family. Unfortunately, things sour between them, and they decide to break up. Who gets the plant? They both can't have it. The woman wants to keep it because she waters it every day; the man wants to keep it because he bought the fertilizer. Neither one of them thought to think this far in advance of what would happen if they broke up. The plant needs them both and is unaware of any issues between its caregivers. Without contributions from both sides, there wouldn't be life. Don't treat your child like a souvenir from a vacation. They need daily care and watering just as much as they need to be rooted in nutrient-rich fertilizer for steady growth. The irresponsibility of couples when it comes to sex is juvenile because the outcome of having sex can be a life. Similar to the plant life, it'll need the sun (mom) and the rain (dad) to survive.

It's a couple's obligation to create a loving, progressive, safe space for their children to grow, and the origin of this all starts with two caring parents.

Emotionally Mental

Emotions are frequently overlooked when people discuss health. It's always presumed that we think we're healthy if we watch our calorie count or sugar intake. But to achieve greater health, it constitutes the entire body and mind. We wonder why people, seemingly healthy and normal, break down and commit heinous crimes or harm themselves. It's an emotional and mental breakdown. As human beings, we have a remarkable brain and even more complex consciousness within that brain that has many layers that can ignite emotions at any given time. We shouldn't ignore them. What we should do is to take the time to detail what emotions we are regularly feeling. This would significantly strengthen our emotional health and create a sense of comfort in our being. We take it for granted when people ask us how we are doing? We'll dismiss it as everyday pleasantries and not an invitation to dump all our emotions in their laps. Imagine if we did that? Responding with our emotional state every time someone asked how we were doing. "I'm feeling lonely this morning, Jane." or "I'm jealous Tom." or I'm envious, I'm hurt, I feel anguish, I'm bitter, I feel contentment, etc. Giving honest, detailed answers of how we are feeling emotionally each time someone asked would be freeing. But at the same time, exhausting to those who have to hear all your unpacked emotions.

As a society, we tend not to spill our emotions onto people as an unspoken favor to them. We reply with readymade responses, sparing them of our potentially upsetting, but honest thoughts. "I'm just fine, and you?" or "I'm well, what about yourself? It's virtually an automatic deflection because we are scared of the responses we'd get if we shared our true feelings. "Are you okay? Is there something wrong? What's got into you?" or better yet, "What's coming out of you?" Dumping our emotions onto people isn't the societal norm so we find it easier to say absolutely nothing about how we feel. Fear keeps us on an emotional auto-pilot when we're in public.

Eventually, our emotions will seep throughout our bodies and egress through our demeanor, actions, and more commonly the way we choose our words. Usually, what we are holding in will always find a way out. Hopefully, it'll be constructively and not de-destructively.

Dealing with different personalities daily, I've come to find that people aren't always okay. It's important to check on your strong friend, your busy friend, your happy friend, your 'seem' to handle everything friend, because even positive people have negative thoughts. They just manage them better. Talking to friends and talking to strangers is much different. Some find it much easier to talk to strangers about what's going on with them emotionally than to speak with their loved ones. People do it all the time in therapy, with a physiatrist, psychologist, doctors, dentist, policemen, lawyers, radio and talk show host, etc. They reveal feelings that require a non- judgmental, unbiased ear to receive it. Usually, we speak to our close friends, family, peers, and people from work about what's bothering us, and that seems to be therapeutic in short bursts, but the backlash of that is, "How will they view me after I tell them?" That's the fear that keeps us captive and refrains us from expressing those rooted emotions to others. As a society, I want to delve into how going to therapy is just as important as going to the gym.

About 47 million adults over the age of 18 cope with some sort of mild mental illnesses. 47 million? If you're not in a room alone, all you have to do is look around, and at least every other person your eyes land-upon has a mental illness. Now, we don't know whether it's mild, moderate, or severe, but what we do know is that it's one of them. So why aren't people more inclined to seek help? I've noticed that the main reason is that they don't know that they even have an illness, which accounts for why half of the people never receive treatment. The second is the fear of the stigma attached. Being labeled mentally incompetent or judged because they sought out help is something that they defiantly don't want. Hence the pushback responses, "I don't have an illness, I'm not sick!" or "There's nothing wrong with me." The misconception about mental illness is that once diagnosed. It's forever.

On the contrary, the brain creates new connections and restructures itself to manage whatever you command it to throughout the course of your life. Plus, mental illness deals with a wide range of disorders that I'm sure we've all experienced at one time or another. An example of one of the major disorders many people suffer from is anxiety. Some of us may feel butterflies before an important speech or moments leading up to a big presentation, but a person who suffers this constant feeling of fear and worry may need some reconstruction in their thinking. Having that constant feeling of angst has to be torturous to that individual. Anxiety affects not only your emotional state, but it alters your behavioral traits as well. When you can't be who you are in fear of the sinking feeling it gives you inside, then your body starts to react to it. This can then begin to interfere with your job, your relationships, your school performance, and your day to day living. Naturally, people feel anxious for a slew of reasons, but my target today is the connection it has to the fatherless and the abandoned. It's an easy bridge for me to connect because that uneasiness of being rejected again as an adult worries them. Due to the fact that in their youth, they were unable to identify their stressors, they, therefore, established a sense of frustration and nervousness that carried into their adulthood. That's anxiety.

Another common illness for the fatherless and abandoned is depression. Depression is one of the most common mental disorders in the United States; to some its referred to as the slow killer, the holy ghost of mental illness. What should not be common is having a constant sinking feeling of hopelessness, dejection, or sadness. Usually, depression is brought by some life-changing event, and losing a father or the rejection of one both qualifies as a life-changer in my book. It can cause a person to lose interest in things they used to find pleasure in, spiraling them into a deep depressed state.

They can begin to lose sleep, have a loss of appetite, loss of concentration, thoughts of self-worth, and low energy. This psychological trauma has imprinted emotional stress that shows up in their adult lives for abandoned children. It affects their decision making, their responses to rejection, their future choices, and their ability to trust others. That feeling of unworthiness, unloved, or feeling defective in some ways can quickly drive a person into a depression. If their particular triggers are ignited, they can withdraw into isolation, become distant, and disconnected without even knowing it. That's why it's crucial to check on your friends, colleagues, relatives, and school mates when they show signs of depression. Sometimes all they need to do is talk it out with someone.

Other mental disorders can be related to abandonment, such as Attention-Deficit/Hyperactivity Disorder, better known as ADHD, where people have difficulty staying focused. Post-Traumatic Stress Disorder or PTSD, this disorder is usually associated with exposure to violence, but not limited to it. It's where people experience a traumatic event that significantly impairs their ability to function at home, at work, and socially. PTSD of abandonment is a separation trauma that can develop after losing a father or even how that father left the family. I remember playing the board game Taboo with a group of friends. It's a verbal game that requires one person to tactfully describe the top word on a small card without using gestures or the word itself and five other taboo words listed. One of my friends was an expert player and gave excellent clues that had us flying through the game all night.

Suddenly, on one amazing run of dishing out clues, he had a long pause, sweat beaded on his forehead, and he began to stammer. Time ran out, and we missed out on a game winning point. When we all learned that the word that stumped him was "cigarette," we all thought that should've been one of the more easier words to describe. Later, he privately shared his story with me, and I then understood. His father left him when he was seven years old, and he recalls every detail of the last time he saw him. He describes the entire scene to me with vivid details, from the smell in the air, the clothes he was wearing, down to the sounds he heard. I can see why he's such a good player in the game like Taboo that rewards excellent description.

In short, one sunny day, his father told his mother that he was going to the corner store for a pack of cigarettes and never returned. He flashes back to his father, waving goodbye to him as he drove past him in his blue '71 El Camino. He said he watched his father's car slowly disappear down a dirt road as billows of dust vanished him from his life. As he recanted his story, the crackling in his voice made it clear to me that the pain he felt as a child has never left him. He holds real resentment towards his father for not only going but also leaving with no explanation, no goodbyes, and no reasons why. The most painful goodbyes are the ones that are never said and never explained. As a result, my friend has separation trauma brought on by this PTSD that continues to trigger him well into his adult life.

Another mental illness that can be brought on by abandonment or fatherlessness is Borderline Personality Disorder or BPD. It's a severe mental disorder marked by patterns of unpredictable verbal or physical outbursts. A person with this type of condition may experience heightened episodes of anger, depression, or anxiety. These experiences often result in a person having impulsive actions to passive situations, leaving the receiver of these actions bewildered and questioning the trigger that brought on that attack.

This disorder is the culprit of many unstable relationships because of the instability in moods and behavior. A prime example of BPD is (Angry Angie). Her anger and violent outburst led me to believe she could be a prime candidate for this disorder. Like Angie and many other people around the world, they don't even realize that they have a mental illness until an intervention is absolutely needed.

It's crucial to know the importance of emotional health and understand it's value. To regulate and monitor your emotions, you must first identify them. What are your healthy and unhealthy emotions? What are the roots of those unhealthy emotions, and how do they affect your actions and reactions? To reach the pinnacle of your personal growth, you must recognize and control your emotions. It will give you a sense of confidence that you would not otherwise have. This will allow peace and well-being to set in, which is a significant part of an individual's mental and emotional health. Fatherless adults can attest to dealing with or having dealt with emotional health such as low self-esteem, anxiety, depression, or self-worth while growing up. Left untreated, those emotions can spawn into something much worse. Identifying what triggers those emotions will help better manage a person's behavior. You may ask, what are the triggers? Anything that reminds, recalls or resurfaces past experiences and the emotions that accompanied them. It can stimulate a persons' brain to have mental reenactments of those abandonment scenarios that haunted them during their childhood. A quick flash from the past can be brought on by a picture, an aroma, a person, a situation, or anything that unearths those past experiences. Those flashbacks are like sticks of dynamite, and your emotions are the highly explosive nitroglycerin packed inside. Your trigger is the fuse, and anything that lights it (i.e., a picture, place, smell, or situation), will set off a catastrophic explosion. Those triggers can send flashback experiences to that individual, and they'll begin to feel emptiness, unworthiness, or unloved feelings they felt as a child. This can unconsciously incite misdirection of those emotions and aim the blame towards others, particularly loved ones. This misdirection or displacement, which is the redirection of pent-up feelings, meant for their absent father. This only delays the healing process and takes them further away from dealing with the after-effects of being raised without a father. They may feel cheated, unwanted, or disposable; those emotions tend to pop up when triggered by something that reminds them of their absent dads and certain parts of their childhood. Understanding your triggers is extremely important to your overall emotional health and healing.

Coping with the sadness of an absent father isn't easy to overcome, but it can be managed. Remember, emotions are thoughts, so if you can change the thought pattern that triggers those self-defeating emotions, you can create a positive thinking habit. Choose constructive thought patterns over destructive thought patterns, and you can naturally counter those emotions. At my leadership camps, I use a technique to demonstrate how to interrupt negative thought patterns. First, I would ask my participants to count in their heads up to 50. I would give them a moment to get into a counting rhythm. I could see them bouncing their heads to numbers and trying to focus. Then I would blurt out random things such as "At a green light, you go, and at a yellow light you slow, so what do you do at a flashing red light?" They would try to answer correctly, and I would immediately ask them what number they left off of. I would get mixed answers, but admittedly none were ever right. They could see how thinking about something can be broken up with speaking aloud and interrupting that particular thought pattern. I tell them not to stay focused on thoughts, schemes, or people that don't benefit their wellbeing, instead break that thought pattern up by concentrating on what's good in their lives or what needs to be done to correct a problem. Responding to a negative post, people, or opinions only keeps them in the same negative space, and growth can never happen there. Children that have deeper issues other than the immediate surface problem are the ones I worry about most. Those children don't have fathers in their lives and are prone to fighting, having a short fuse, refusing help, or disobeying authority.

I advise those children not to remain stuck on that fatherless merry-go-round of responses throughout their lives. Things change, life changes, and so can they. Change comes with knowing that those emotions originated from their childhood, and they don't have to live in that loop of heartbreaking moments forever. It's like watching a scary movie over and over again; the more you replay it and familiarize yourself with the surprises, the less you'll be frightened. You begin to develop numbness to the parts of the movie that triggered fright in you the first time you saw it, the same works with dealing with fatherlessness as a young adult. The moment you recognize the connection between your emotions and childhood, you'll begin to take your power back. You'll be able to put a voice to the pain, verbalizing your truth. As the saying goes, "The truth shall make you free." You can now free yourself of those unhealthy emotions and begin to experience healthy ones that can only benefit your life for the rest of your life.

It's totally understandable for adults who felt like or were abandoned in their youth to feel anxiety and depression. The goal is to process those feelings to reach a place of resolve by diagnosing those triggers. Therapy can assist with that. Therapeutic counseling is perfect for individuals experiencing hopelessness and desperation. It allows truth to be spoken aloud and heard by the author of those words. It enables them to become vulnerable when they share their true feelings from that wounded heart. When this is done, it'll bring relief to the person's inner peace, and inner peace is ground zero of emotional and mental wellness.

Life changes us. Children change us. Health changes us. Our jobs change us. Our friends change us. Growing older changes us. The only thing that stays constant is the unavoidable obstacles that we will endure throughout our lives. We must always be prepared to hurdle those obstacles with grace and confidence. The day I met and heard ROAD RAGE RICK's story in Counselor Danita's sessions taught me that everybody doesn't handle obstacles the same way. Throughout his life, Rick's ways of handling problems have only landed him behind bars, the loss of his daughter, the loss of jobs, income, and today a loss of his time. Road Rage Rick is a truck driver in his late 40's. He shares custody of his thirteen-year-old daughter with an ex-girlfriend. When he's not on the road, he lives in his brother-in-law's guest house in Modesto, California. Rick smokes a pack a day, he pops pills to stay awake on long road trips, and when he's home, he drinks excessively. When he speaks, it's loud, boisterous, and all over the place. He feels America owes him something for merely existing and gets annoyed by the slightest offenses. About two years ago, he was arrested for assault and battery of a man at a bar and spent some time in jail. He was charged recently with domestic violence against his daughter's mother for spitting in her face because she denied him visitation. It's no secret why Road Rage Rick needs anger management, and I want to find out if it has anything to do with his childhood. Let's get into one of his sessions and shed some light on how his childhood and growing up fatherless may have played a role in his life thus far.

COUNSELOR - How was everybody's weekend?

Rick wasted no time and went straight into what happened to him over the weekend. He says while on the highway, this guy screamed at him, gave him an obscene gesture, and then had the gall to follow him off the exit. He says that he and the guy got into a heated exchange on the side of the road, a typical case of road rage, hence his name.

ROAD RAGE RICK - This guy was begging for a beating. I was well within my rights to punch him in his face, but I held my composure and only kicked his car as the chicken shit sped off.

Rick laughs. The group chuckled as well, but the Counselor and I were concerned.

COUNSELOR - Kicking his car was an act of aggression and really bad behavior on your part. Although the guy was wrong to follow you and provoke you, we are only speaking of what you could have done to have left that scene unscathed. What other decisions could you have made or choices you could have chosen to have kept you from that boiling point?

Rick's answer was the classic deflection, and it took another twenty minutes to get him to admit to his responsibility of it all.

COUNSELOR - People, we all have triggers. It's our responsibility to identify and contain them.

She uses everyone's situation as an example to teach the class how to handle their situation. She then focused back on Rick and asked him about his upbringing. He tells a story of how his mom used to get beaten by his dad in drunken rages, how his father would rather be with his motorcycle buddies than be home with him and his siblings. Rick says his father didn't care too much for family life, so he wasn't around. His neglectful mom and her many boyfriend's raised Rick. Trying to find love herself, many boyfriends courted her and attempted to connect with little Rick on some level during the courtship. Neither they nor their efforts ever felt genuine to Rick. Those men wanted his mom and not him, because once his mother was done with them, so was their fake love for him. Up until this point in Rick's fragile life, he had good reason not to put his trust in men, so he didn't. The problem with this is that he never learned how to communicate, discuss, and bond with men. Having a responsible father around would have shown him this through their examples.

ROAD RAGE RICK - I remember I got suspended for setting all the extinguishers off in the school. The school wanted my parents to replace the units or face charges. They couldn't reach my dad, so my mother came on my behalf. She was upset and concerned. She told them that my dad was off working somewhere, but she and I both knew we hadn't seen him in years. I sat there, listening to the same lie about my father for 14 years. Maybe I was looking for more attention from him in this, but as they say, when you look for something, don't be surprised at what you'll find. I remember my mom and I seeing him out on his bike, and we stopped him. I was in the back seat of the car and heard them talking about me and my behavior. He could give a rats ass what I did. He just stood there, shrugging his shoulders, and didn't even come to the car to speak to me. He didn't even have the decency to give me a nod, just a blank expression. He didn't care.

COUNSELOR - Did his reaction disappoint you?

ROAD RAGE RICK - He made me feel like I wasn't his problem. Like, it didn't matter to him; I didn't matter to him. So, the hell with it!

Like many other neglected children, Road Rage Rick tried getting his father's attention by acting out. When that failed, he began to turn his frustration onto others. This is where bullies are made. Children don't know any better if they're not shown the way. Well into his adult life, he's still negatively looking for attention. During those sessions, Rick made it excruciatingly difficult for Counselor Danita to help him at every turn. Without guardian guidance, he mastered the art of self-sufficiency and emotional detachment. He pretty much raised himself, and because of that, he only trusted himself. He didn't acquire many friends along his way to adulthood but made people pay attention to him, regrettably by his behavior. Rick completely disavowed any appearance of neediness and felt as though needing help equaled weakness. As she questioned him, he'd constantly interrupt her and challenged every point made. Attempting to thwart her assessment, he would inch to his seat's edge and deepened his tone as he spoke. She didn't budge; she kept calm and continued to give her feedback. His behavior is read as an intimidation tactic or defense mechanism that he probably recurrently uses to avoid vulnerability. His guards were completely up against her, and watching her tear them down made it very uncomfortable to observe.

She eventually got him to calm down and listen to her evaluation. In a nutshell, she told him that trying to dominate or feel the need to control every situation is unnecessary when you know that you're not broken. She assured him that he was not the problem, but his responses were. Road Rage Rick has a lot of his father in him, and although his father was absent, he mirrors his traits. You ask, if his father wasn't around, then how could he be just like him? And shouldn't he be better without his abusive father around? Both are valid questions, and some would argue that children are better off without toxic and abusive fathers in their lives. His absence was also absent from all the chaos, toxicity, and disruption he brought with him. Although it's easy to agree with this line of thinking, not having a father will still stir up commotion in the heart. Even in his disrespectful, devaluing absence, the child will still be psychologically influenced by the traumas he caused. Simply understanding the fact that it was the father that was toxic and not the child, can most defiantly start the healing process from those past traumas. It will also help the person not to repeat those same mistakes with their own children.

Counselor Danita urges Rick not to take on those bad traits of his father. He doesn't have to be demeaning, threatening, judgmental, or violent to get people to understand him. That's toxic! Instead of just agreeing with her, his narcissism wouldn't allow him to appear not be in control.

As they continued, he switched topics about his work, but Danita brought him back to discuss the incident with the mother of his child and his daughter.

ROAD RAGE RICK - I guess I'd be wrong if I left my daughter because I can't get along with my ex.?

Of course, this exchange between them was only a deflection of feelings on Rick's part, and she ended up giving him a multitude of tools that would help him in his situation with his daughter.

Counselor Danita and I both felt sure that Rick wasn't going to abandon his daughter. He was merely hurting. Now don't get me wrong, hurt people make bad decisions all the time, but Rick was only making that declaration to protect his feelings. Even though he was speaking in hypothetical's, I found it more concerning why he said that instead of what he actually wanted to say. It was another way of protecting his vulnerability by threatening withdrawal. His sarcasm to disconnecting from his daughter to hurt his ex is the same disconnection he felt by his father. Again, this is another case of hurt people hurting people. Their usual mode of operation is to hurt others first, then harden their hearts to pretend they're not hurting themselves.

Road Rage Rick's hurt was speaking loud and clear. He was projecting his hurt outward when all the hurt was inside of him. He's not alone in this; most men look outside themselves for the source of their pain while women tend to look within. Men would say, "You hurt me, so I hurt you." While women feel like, "I hurt you because you hurt me." In the end, it's the same cycle of hurt being set into motion. Hurting people need to search within to locate the source of their pain and corral those emotions into a manageable operating place. Whatever the feeling or emotion, ask yourself, why do I feel that way? What do I do with that feeling? And lastly, where does that feeling come from? Dig deep and answer honestly. This will be a way to begin to understand yourself and why you are the way you are. You will start to fill that hole in your heart, one shovelful at a time.

One way to identify the origin of your trauma is to call it out by its name. For example, "I'm hurt because..." or "I feel this way because..." then once you've identified where the hurt came from, start the healing process by using positive reinforcing statements about yourself, "I am worthy because..." "I'm loved because..." and "I'm no longer staying in this hurt place because..." Do not let your past predict your future, and don't allow people to hold you to your past. Stay away from bullies; people who constantly shame you. Antagonist, people who fight against your change and haters who keep reminding you of who you used to be, instead of applauding who you are becoming. Please don't give them any ground. Push back against what they're saying about you, even if they believe it to be true. Change must occur with ourselves first before we can make changes to how we deal with others. Years ago, I read a book titled "THE FOUR AGREEMENTS" by Don Miguel Ruiz, and it's still one of my favorite reads. In the book, the author speaks about self-worth and accepting or deflecting what people say about you. From those pages, I learned that a person doesn't have to take it personally or, in other words, agree with the opinions of others in order for them to validate themselves. When someone calls you a name or negatively labels you, you allow what they said about you to affect you by taking it personally, or agreeing with their opinion,

You don't have to agree with their opinion. It's merely their opinion of you. It's only when you believe what they've said about you to be true that your emotions are triggered. Most times, what others say about you is a projection of their own reality, not yours. The Four Agreements also taught me that we shouldn't make assumptions about ourselves or others. Clearly, express what you want from yourself or others, which will prevent any misunderstandings, potential sadness, and needless drama. Most of us have agreements that we've adopted from our parents, which isn't bad. Most of them align with how we feel anyway, but their agreements aren't our agreements. You are allowed to choose whatever it is you agree with and what you do not.

Don't let others define you. If you believe their positive assessments of you, then you'll believe their negative ones too. That gives them power to hurt you if you choose to accept their agreements. Again, choose wisely on what it is you accept to be downloaded into your emotional databank. What you say to yourself and about yourself is what creates the emotions that control your behavior. Always speak positive to yourself, be honest with yourself, and don't lie to yourself. You are who you are. Love yourself and take inventory on what you attach to your life and what you must discard from it. Monitor your mental and emotional state by keeping in check those false beliefs of yourself that conjure up from the past.

"We are products of our past, but we don't have to be prisoners of it." - Rick Warren from A Purpose Driven Life: What on Earth Am I Here for?

Choice? Homosexuality/Sexuality Promiscuity

Fathers play an irreplaceable role in children's lives, and that's a fact. However, there are tremendous concerns that the absence of one could have major effects on a person's sexual adaption. Hold up, wait a minute, stop the presses, pause.

I know there are many things that society blames on the absent father, but how in the world can we say, a fatherless home contributes to a person possibly being gay? I've overheard water cooler talk, heated discussions, and friendly debates among colleagues about homosexuality, and it never fails that someone would ask about the father's involvement. What's the connection with that? Could a father's presence prevent or promote a child becoming gay? A few researchers believe that it holds some credence, while others doubt that it plays any part what so ever to a person's sexual orientation. A 1983 study conducted by the Family Research Institute did find a correlation between a person's desire to be homosexual and poor relationships with their fathers. I do believe that there's some weight to not having a father around and what happens to them during their childhood shapes who they'll become as adults. During the AID's epidemic, it was discovered that twice as many black males relative to white males were homosexual and more than double were bisexual.

If you ask me, I will deduce that it was due to genetic predisposition and that an overwhelming percentage of black children were being raised in fatherless homes. I don't want to turn this into a white versus black thing, because at this point it's a children's thing. I'll save the disparities between races for a later chapter when I speak on its effects on the black and brown communities.

People can't choose their fathers, just like they can't choose their race or gender. That's an immutable fact. The homosexual community strongly believes that being homosexual is not a choice but an inborn event. Scientists and religious theologians will debate this matter for eons, but I don't have that kind of time. I'll just say this. I remember a preacher saying, "Do not agree with others sins in order not to offend. Stay in your truth and stand by it." With that said, I don't intend to be insensitive to the arguments of if a person is born gay or if it's a lifestyle choice or even if it's natural or not.

My only objective here is to layout how fatherlessness can directly or indirectly be why some children inadvertently choose their sexual identities. How they think about themselves in terms of who they're attracted to can be traced back to their childhood and possibly clarify who they are and who they're not. I am well aware of the LGBTQ+ arguments of DNA and genes, such as Epigenetics, the study of how external factors can alter the expression of an organism's genes, or basically how a person is born gay. However, I'm not here to argue those points. I'm not here to argue at all. I'm simply suggesting that children can be more vulnerable to molestation, pedophilia, or rape when there's no steady father in the home. Again, I'm only drawing a line between an in-home father and a father living outside of the home. I'm not deliberating those special cases where the parent was the perpetrator or the enabler of those heinous acts.

On the surface, having a father in the home could divert potentially harmful situations that a child could be placed in. A father would teach his son how to protect their physical bodies and teach his daughter how to protect her emotional wellbeing. He can demonstrate what genuine love looks like from a safe place without conditions. Some children who weren't raised by a father may lack emotional awareness in men's presence and mistake their lustful appetence as honest feelings. Sexual deviants disguise lust with love all the time, and without a father to share with or show them what it looks like may help them find themselves, more times than not, in those potentially harmful situations. I want this to be crystal clear; it's never the child's fault. There's absolutely nothing a child could do to have any blame in what a sexual deviant does to them. With that said, one of the ways a person can be confused about their sexual identity can stem from episodes of molestation, pedophilia, and or rape before their teen ages. One in every four girls and 1 in 6 boys will be sexually abused before 18. Exposure to those type of crimes will defiantly alter their natural balance of emotional, physical, sexual, and romantic attraction to others. In 2020 during the beginning of the world's pandemic and subsequent lockdown and stay at home orders due to COVID-19, the National Crime Agency revealed that online sexual abuse increased, and children were under substantial exploitation threats.

The National Society for the Prevention of Cruelty to Children (NSPCC) recorded over 69,000 sexual offenses against children in 2019. The NSPCC reports that a child is sexually abused every 7 minutes.

For an individual sexually violated during the early development stages of their life will be extremely traumatic and confusing.

Children don't know how to feel; they don't understand what's happening to them; all they know is that they want it to stop. In efforts to prevent future traumas, they will avoid anything that reminds them of that traumatic event. They'll tend to behave differently, dress differently, or become different if that would keep them from ever being abused again. If these changes in their behavior can be intercepted early on, it can aid in suppressing ongoing effects as an adult and possibly bring them back into balance with themselves. If not addressed, the residue of sexual abuse can carry over into their adult relationships and how they behave within them. It's strange, but at times the results of that childhood trauma can actuate the abused to engage in physical, emotional, or sexually abusive relationships and not always as the victim, but as the actual abuser. If you think babies having babies is bad, try imagining the sexually abused now being the sexual abusers.

Why is sexual abuse important to note when discussing the topic of homosexuality and children? Here's one reason, in 1970, the Kinsey Institute conducted a study. It resulted in strong patterns to the practice of homosexuality with groups whose first sexual experience was that of the homosexual nature. NSPCC further states that a child's first sexual experiences can resolutely be associated with their adult behavior. On that basis, I conclude that early sexual abuse plays a significant part in a person's sexual identity and their ability to separate that trauma, confusing their feelings and emotions for a same-sex partner.

Children would either replay their trauma over and over in their minds, similar to a war veteran with PTSD, or children would hide the event deep inside as if it hadn't happened. They'll disassociate themselves from it and treat the episode like a distant dream that didn't happen in real life. These things can change a person's sense of identity. Imagine a child that's barely learning bonds, barriers, and boundaries being accosted by a relative, authority figure, or someone of trust. That act may cause them to associate that crime to the entire gender.

As far as I'm concerned, that wouldn't be a far reach to believe that that experience may have altered their sexual identities. We know that feminine and masculine traits are behaviors that are copied, and homosexuality is feelings of sexual attraction towards the same sex. Can homosexuality be a copied behavior? Can it be something or someone they've observed and copied? Perhaps, maybe not, but I believe that exposure to a young boys' feminine traits or a young girl's masculine ones by an experienced homosexual can give that child temporary comfort in something they believed to be coming from a safe and honest place. This comfortability may lead them to choose that lifestyle for solidarity and safety. Is homosexuality a choice? Some would say that it isn't a choice similar to race and gender, but then others would debate it and come to the summation that it's copied behaviors. Who do we believe? Can behaviors be inherited? We know disease and physical traits can, but behaviors? Possibly. If enough of those behaviors were observed over a long period, it's a strong probability. For the sake of clarity, I want to separate the two. On the one hand, we have people who believe that people are born homosexual, and then on the other hand, some believe it's a chosen lifestyle, whether by way of environment, influence, or abuse. In this case, I want to speak to those who are not claiming to be born with the homosexual desire, but to those who later adopted that desire.

Homosexual desire can come from any one of these ways:

1. Any homosexual experience in childhood, especially if it is a first sexual experience.

2. Any homosexual contact with an adult, particularly with a relative or authority figure.

3. An absent, distant, or rejecting father.

4. Exposure to pornography early in childhood or sexual interaction with adult males.

5. Pro-homosexual sex education and their cultural influences.

I don't want to be insensitive to those who've been through sexual trauma, but concerning this list, number 3 is the only one that doesn't have sex, the act of sex, or the desire of sex connected to it. This was so important to include on this list by the experts who have already concluded that these are the strongest possibilities to the path of homosexuality. For young girls, an absent, distant, or rejecting father will leave her emotionally broken and struggling with self-worth. She will often try to compensate by dressing immodestly, using too much make-up, or being sexually subjective on social media. If a man sexually abused her, she may become more masculine in order to hide her femininity to avoid any unwanted sexual attention from males. Afraid to be herself and living a lie. This camouflaging of her true self confuses her and can easily become a lifestyle in her young adulthood. Not knowing her father can be a huge component in her living a promiscuity life or one of homosexuality. Now, I'm still a strong believer that behavior is a choice, and at some point, each one of us has the free will to change our minds, our position, and our lives.

With that said, for little boys without fathers in the home, all they can do is watch, emulate and become. What do I mean by that? The effects of a fatherless home are different for little girls and little boys. Girls can watch and mirror their mothers on becoming a woman, whereas little boys have no man to observe. His first feminine behavior traits come from being surrounded by femininity, not necessarily a gene he was born with. He's subjected to watching, listening, and learning from feminine programming in the home, female teachers at school, his mother, aunt, sisters and their girlfriends. It's not uncommon for a young boy that's encompassed in this female environment to display a few female mannerisms. Children are like sponges soaking up everything, so they want to be like the adults surrounding them. They want to talk like them, move like them and sometimes dress like them. It's innocent and child-like, but it can become confusing if left unchecked. Don't blame the child; question the adults around them. Just because the little boy wants to play dress up in his mommies clothes doesn't mean he's gay. He's innocent. With correction, he'll have understanding. Just because a little girl wants to do everything little boys do (tomboy) doesn't mean she wants to be lesbian; she needs reassurance that it's okay to compete as a girl. Children aren't thinking about sex at those young ages; they're just trying to find their place in a world that gave them no father presence in their lives. A father's presence will give a visual template on how a man is supposed to be, and a detached or inadequate father will only damage that child's impression of one.

There's Your Side, My Side, and Suicide

Week seven started with me inching along in California traffic, sipping green tea with a little French vanilla creamer. I'm in no hurry, no radio, no phone calls, just me and my thoughts. Before I left home, the local news began to run a story about a young girl committing suicide, I didn't get the whole story, so my thoughts were on this little girl, why, how and what for? What could cause a person, a child no less, to take their own life? Mental illness? A cry for help? I was curious, so I turned onto the news radio broadcast to perhaps hear more about the story. It didn't take long; the story of this young girl took over the airways. The spin on it was suicide because of bullying. The news covered the story in detail and, like clockwork, added several similar stories along with statistics, demographics, and solutions. The journalist asked the people what should be done and how we can stop this from happening again.

The girl was only nine years old, and she couldn't take the teasing and badgering anymore. Growing up, we've all been bullied on some level, but as young children, we don't understand that the world is much bigger than our bullies. Adults understand it a bit better but still fall short of truly realizing that people will say cruel things to feel better about themselves. Bullies are cowards that are afraid to simply be themselves. If, as a child, you were bullied and did nothing about it, nine times out of ten, you're probably susceptible to be bullied again. Either through cyber-bullying, bullied by a boss, a co-worker, or strangers. You believe you've survived the bullying because you did nothing, but doing nothing only hibernated your confrontation. I was taught to face a bully head-on, win or lose, it must be done, here and now. Others can attest to this; facing your bully will be life-changing and rewarding in the long run. Parents usually protect their children from harm, but away from home, they can't help, but they can teach their children to stand up for themselves. Moma bears confront the bully, while fathers will teach their child how to protect themselves from bullies.

For young boys, a father will support a young man to help him defend himself. For little girls, the dad will support and protect her by being there, such as walking her to school hand in hand, answering harassing phone calls from jealous friends, and visiting the child's parents who are doing the bullying. Mothers can do the same, but there's nothing like having that strength of a man stepping in to put a cease to any physical threat to his children. Being demeaned to the point of demise is a terrible thing and for those who bully are probably products of bullying themselves.

Children emulate what's at home. When I arrived at Counselor Danita's office, I had to ride up the elevator with a couple of people, including Baby Moma Monique. They were talking about the sad story of this young girl's suicide. When the three of us exited the elevator, Counselor Danita was outside her office having a private moment with Road Rage Rick. Our suicide conversation continued as we walked past and entered the session.

Monique took off her scarf and coat then sat comfortably on the couch, which was part of our semi-circle of chairs. I stood near the table of coffee and donuts. I shared the preceding news of the day, and we all had thoughts on it. Everybody was engaging and had something to add. I noticed a girl in her named Susan, aka SUICIDE SUSAN (white, mid-'20s), not engaging or saying anything. She was already in the room, head down, cupping her styrofoam coffee cup with both hands. I directed my statement towards her to get her involved, "I believe everyone has a bullying story, and most come out of it unscathed, but it's never forgotten." Suicide Susan looks up from staring into her coffee cup and in a soft voice shares her battle with suicide as a teenager. Through my observation Susan was a very quiet person; her demeanor was un-engaging and timid. When asked to share her thoughts or perspectives, she'd often drop her head in her hands and politely pass. There's something about therapy that invites people to open up to total strangers, but not loved ones. It's a safe and nonjudgmental space.

Once a participant feels safe and free from judgment, their wall of defense is broken down. On several occasions, Counselor Danita would ask Susan to engage in the group talk, but she would quickly close up and shut down. She reminds me of a turtles, the way her head would recoil back into her shoulders when she was asked to speak. For some reason, today she had something to add. I sat down and picked up my pen and pad. The turtle's head was about to peek. This was undoubtedly a rare moment. I believe everyone understood the importance of her breakthrough. No one interrupted or dared to add a comment. It was like we were all frozen, afraid to make any sudden moves that could cause her to recede back into her shell's safety. Her story took us through her childhood and how her parents were deeply in love and poured their love into her. Outside of the general no smoking, drinking, or sexual activity, she revealed how she was raised in a very narrow and sheltered environment. Her mother didn't allow hanging out after school or invite friends over, and being on the internet was forbidden.

Back then, some parents were hesitant about subjecting their children to the evils of the internet. Imagine that in today's world. Most parents would agree that the core standards that were set for Susan are no different than their very own. Unfortunately, sheltering children from society introverts them and inevitably drives them to push their edge. Susan's recluse demeanor always appeared to be timid, so I was anxious to hear about her edge. She recounts, "My mother taught me a lot of things, presuppositions were built-in, but a lot. She wanted me to be a paralegal or something, something safe. Her expectations of what she wanted me to be disappointed her when I decided to be a tattoo artist." We did not see that coming. She didn't seem to be the quintessential tattoo artist, with no visible tattoos, a bunch of piercings, or even an edgy hairstyle for that matter.

Nothing pointed to her being a tattoo artist. On the cover, she looked like a person that have been sheltered her whole life, but I know that sheltered people can sometimes be reckless.

They would try to make up for the lost time, taking chances they wouldn't normally take. Not, Susan, she's been telling her story with little eye contact and occasionally looking up from her hands that were in her lap. She would quickly look away the moment she caught eye contact with someone in the room.

As much in love her parents were, her mother couldn't save her father from being a habitual drunk driver. According to Susan's mother, her father left work after arguing with her over finances. He went to a local bar, got drunk and on his way home he sideswiped a car and cascaded into the guard rail, flipping his car over onto oncoming traffic. He was ejected and died on impact.

Susan was six years old when this happened. Her mom blames herself and believes that he purposely took his life over mounting debt because of the families' escalating finances. "I know I have anger problems, and sometimes I'm not fair to people because I feel like life wasn't fair to me. I have a hard time making friends. I push them away when they talk about their dads and spending time with them. I feel awkward, pretending to be happy for them." Susan adds. She would often run away from home, experiment with drugs, opioids, in particular, to drown out the noise in her life. The noise only got louder as she tried to navigate through her teenage years. Like most teenagers that feel inept, she despised going to school. Kids would pick on her all the time.

It was a torturous task walking through a gauntlet of insults, giggles, and whispers down the hallways. We all know school can be hard, but for the socially awkward, it can be a nightmare. Trying to avoid any threat that jeopardizes or exposes their self-appointed awkwardness can be suicidal in itself. Susan felt as though she didn't fit in any of the socially accepted groups. For a timid skinny teenager, it could be the most insignificant reason on the surface, but immensely valid to her to conclude that taking her own life is her only solution. Bullying and taunting by students and irresponsible adults-only compounded her lack of confidence. Susan's mothers attempted to minimize her daughter's risk by sheltering her, but instead, it created doubt, fear, and uncertainty.

Children who are constantly rescued from distress cannot develop resiliency and a type of toughness needed in this world. In attempts to reduce her anxiety from her husband's tragic loss, Susan's mother discouraged her from taking any risk to protect her from every stressful situation she could. This is a hard one because 99% of all parents would implement rules and guidelines to keep their children from harm, but in Susan's upbringing, it backfired.

Susan never gained the confidence and perseverance needed to handle bullies; they found her awkwardness an easy target. To this day, Susan constantly avoids any type of criticism because it gives her high anxiety. She self-medicates then reverts to sulking in her self-loathing and depression. This is the state of mind where her suicidal thoughts germinate and gain ground over her salubrious thoughts. Susan is no different than many teens across America. Suicide is the second leading cause of death for people between the ages of 10 and 25, and from that, four out of five will attempt to give warning signs. Many of those signs are missed, ignored, or made light of by irresponsible adults. Susan came dangerously close to falling in the 63 percentile of fatherless children who commit suicide. Children that lose a father in their early stages of development feel the effects similar to abandonment. The difference is abandonment is a forced separation, and death is a permanent one.

SUICIDE SUSAN - The things I went through at school was

criminal. I was so traumatized that I skipped school a lot. Losing my father made me feel alone, and kids at school all had fathers. I had no more dad, no one to pick me up or no one to run to when I was scared. I was alone.

She buried her chin in her chest and stopped talking. She began to fiddle with a piece of loose thread on her sleeve. It seemed like forever that we all sat in her silence. No one uttered a word, cleared their throat, or adjusted their seat. We all were sensitive to her emotions that were clear as day, then she picked up her head and continued,

SUICIDE SUSAN - I didn't want a fake father in my life; when my mom started to date, I would ignore her boyfriends. I wouldn't talk to them or take their gifts or even look at them. I wouldn't allow myself to connect with any of them on any level. I was a pretty rotten kid because I wasn't ready to replace my dad so easily, like my mom was.

Grief is a very long process to get over, and dealing with a parent's death is difficult to endure. It brings separation and the feeling of finalization. For Suicide Susan, she wasn't ready to put a period at the end of her father's story. When her mother tried to move on with finding another relationship, it became apparent that it was an emotion-laden event for them both every single time. Children inherently do not want to replace their parents, and anything that threatens that will experience some resistance. The death of a parent can be dealt with, but it takes time, support, and patience.

COUNSELOR - Susan, your father's death wasn't your mother or your fault. It's very common for the people left behind to blame each other and begin fighting among each other to feel relief. This is blame-shifting. People grieve differently and, most times, on separate timelines. Like in your case, your grieving period wasn't complete, and that's understandable. But you can't hold others to your same grieving timeline. When people assume this, it can cause major conflict among family members.

Susan takes that in and then continues,

SUICIDE SUSAN - It did put a wedge between my mother and me. I haven't let that go, and I know it's affecting my life now in some wicked way.

COUNSELOR - Were some of the issues you had with your mother over your father?

SUICIDE SUSAN - Defiantly, it was brought up quite often when we argued. I was about 16, and I couldn't take it anymore, the bullying, not having my father, not getting along with my mother. The world seemed so small, and I was too big to be in it. I didn't fit. I felt I had only two choices: swallow a bottle of pills or run away. I did both; I left home like I was going to school and never came back home. My plan was to just get lost, but my plan didn't work out because it was cold and I didn't bring enough warm clothes. All I had was those pills; I wanted to take them, fall asleep, and end it all.

She began to stammer. Baby Moma Monique offered comfort by rubbing her knee. The whole group added sympathetic support and was very reassuring. This had to be hard for Susan to conjure up and share her story, but I felt a wonderful sense of warmth, witnessing all the participants' support.

SUICIDE SUSAN - I thought about all the hurtful things the kids would say and do to me. I was different, and I knew it. If enough people say it about you, it must be true, right? Then I thought about my father's death, and I begin to cry. I gripped that bottle so hard that the sweat from my palms made the label lose its elasticity.

COUNSELOR - At that moment, you were multiplying your depression by recalling all the bad and ignoring the good.

Susan looks up.

SUICIDE SUSAN - For some reason, I wanted it that way. I wanted somebody to feel sorry for me, I suppose. I wanted to show people how cruel they were to me. I wanted to show them. I wanted to get back at them for hurting me. No one cared about me, so why should I? I didn't care anymore.

COUNSELOR - The only thing you would have proven if you had completed that. You would have never known how important you were to your community. Life happens, and it happens to all of us. It comes in quarters. You can't quit it in the first or second quarter, because the third and fourth quarter can be the best quarters in your entire life. Today is not tomorrow, and tomorrow there's always potential. Potential love, potential change, potential growth. Where did you find yourself at that moment?

SUICIDE SUSAN - I was alone. I swallowed the pills two at a time until the bottle was empty and sat down.

Crying and yelling at the top of my lungs at the trees in the park. I pretended they were the people that hurt me. I cursed then, but at the same time, I believed what they said about me. I wanted to die. I fell asleep until someone on the street found me and called the police. Three days in the hospital, two stomach pumps and an I.V drip later, I was back at home in my bed with my mom crying over me.

Suicide Susan's story is a prime example of two of the effects of a fatherless home. As mentioned before, 63% commit suicide, and 90% run away from home. Consider the statistics that for every successful suicide in America (around 40,000), there are 25 failures. Thank God Suicide Susan was unsuccessful in her attempt. She's still struggling with her confidence and depression levels, but she's better than she was. As a teen, she could not express the overwhelming feeling of loss or discharge all the emotions she had stored up. Susan was a person that didn't deal with death directly, but instead indirectly with her silence. Being silent in times when she needs to be heard can severely hinder her emotional health and development. Shutting down or fleeing was her defense mechanism of choice. Her running away from home as a teenager morphed into her running away in her adulthood. Such as her work, her commitments, schooling, relationships, and any other circumstance where she felt a strong possibility of criticism. Suicide Susan and people like her should not be overlooked as quiet people. Chances are there was some catastrophic event that tilted their childhood balance and stymied their confidence. That's why therapy is so important. It gives people a place for openness and the ability to put a voice to store up emotions.

The effects of losing a father infected Susan with suicidal thoughts and ill intent, but like others in the fatherless community, it's something that must be addressed and treated.

Some irresponsible adults and insensitive people would say, "Get over it.". When it comes to a loss of life, it's extremely difficult to simply, "Get over." Losing a father has a much more potent effect on children than incarceration or divorce. The dynamics are different because this fatherless group can never meet, find, or reach out to the man responsible for their existence ever again. They are truly fatherless children. They may remember their father's voice like a catchy song, but because it was early in their childhood, that song is riddled with missing lyrics. I can personally connect to the consequences of losing a parent early on when I was 13, a good friend from my neighborhood lost his dad. It hurt the community because he was one of the active fathers in our neighborhood. He was a hard-working, authoritative, caring man that lived with his wife and children. He was always at our baseball games and a very supportive father. Not just to my friend, but to all of the kids in the hood. When he passed away, my friend took it pretty hard, and it changed him. I remember it being the first funeral I attended, and I didn't like it one bit. Who would? I stayed outside and listened in from the steps. I was scared to see a dead body. As time went on, we all could see that his fathers' death changed him. He just didn't care anymore. He quit our baseball team and start hanging out with the older and tougher kids in the neighborhood. He started picking fights and being more of a menace to the community. My friend, soon after, dropped out of school. Most fatherless children don't become educational failures, but most educational failures are fatherless children.

He never returned to school, and from there it was a quick downward spiral through the court and penal systems. His life never really recovered from there. I'm sad to say that he was just finishing up an eight-year prison sentence the last time I went back to the old neighborhood. Losing a father affects human beings' biology. It changes their DNA. For a young boy, losing his living example forces him to become a man much sooner than expected. He's laden with more responsibilities and earlier than anticipated form of independence. For young girls, their sexuality can be defined by the relationship she has with her father. Losing him can cause her to be more sexually active earlier in life than she normally would with a father in the home.

This is the hardest chapter I had to write because, during the writing of this book, and this chapter in particular, I lost the man that I knew as my father. He was the rock of our family and the strength in our togetherness. As I proofread this chapter, I began to cry, thinking of my father. I feel hurt, numbness, and a tremendous loss. As far as it having long-term effects on the trajectory in my life it has yet to be seen. This book is to connect with adults that grew up in fatherless homes. Although I had a father in my life, the only father that played with me, clothed me, loved me, reprimanded me, consoled me, and gave me direction. I still think about the biological father that gave me life, and as a child, I cried for his absence, but when I lost the only father that I knew and the only father that raised me, I knew what mourning meant. Even as I go through the preparations to lay my father to rest, I can't help but wonder where I would have been without him. Of course, I'm affected by knowing that my biological father didn't want me, but now that my step-up father is no longer here to talk to me, it hurts more than I can write in words. Those who lost a parent knows what I'm going through, but the loss of a parent is something that changes you and changes the definition of your story. No more visits to dad or calling your dad or asking your dad what he thinks. He's gone. For those who never had a father in their lives carries this pain, but it's not the same. An absent father is just that, absent. He's around, but not around you. With the death of a father, there are no other options. He's unreachable forever—that true un-fillable hole.

DIVORCE: The Ultimate Divide and Conquer

Julius Caesar once said, "Divida et Impera," which translates to "Divide and Rule." In family courts all across America, families are being divided and ruled upon by the strict outdated laws of the land. It's fairly easy to get married, but very costly to get a divorce. The only thing that stays constant is the court's high cost. The complications of dividing all the assets, who gets custody of the children, alimony payments, the ugliness of in-court battles against each other are all a part of dissolving a marriage, but dissolving a family should be held in the higher court of moral opinion. To do the right thing by the children should be the number one goal of the spouses. It's not only the divorce that tears families apart; it's what takes place during the court proceedings. Lies, secrets, accusations, blame, betrayal, animosity, etc. It sounds like the opening logline to a raunchy reality show, with insults and drinks being slung at each other. In a divorce, couples surprisingly find out what each partner really thinks about the other. Things that were lingering underneath, but wasn't spoken or was spoken, but not heard. In either case, the outcome was the same. Can a couple with divorce aspirations marriage be salvaged? Yes, it can, but it'll take a lot of work, and people usually don't believe love in relationships should be work, so they bailout. The American court system will gladly take your money to go through with it; they aren't there to give you marriage counseling. The family court is there to make sure the separation is fair and that the children are okay. It's easier to get a marriage license than a driver's license and much harder than both of them to get a divorce. I wonder why people would rather divorce than work through their problems. Of course, each case is unique, but there are too many cases that the reasons for divorce are as little as, "He snores." Saving marriages isn't my book's focus, but I wished couples would stay together. If couples want out, then why shouldn't they be able to leave? Well, they can, and they do. The problem is that the children are left behind to make sense of why mommy and daddy don't love each other anymore. And if they can stop loving each other, will they eventually stop loving me? In this chapter, I want to stay focused on the children who are now adults, raised in a fatherless home because of divorce. It's too late to go back and change the outcome, but it's never too late to change the thinking of those affected. One thing the courts don't do, and that's raise the kids after they finalize the parties' separation. The courts are more concerned about the bottom line and each entity that gets paid from a divorce. It makes breaking up more profitable than keeping marriages together. The incentive is to make money, not make marriages. The family courts make more money than any other courts combined. Criminal, traffic, civil or small claims. I owned and operated a driving school in California for a number of years, and in my business, I spent many hours in and out of traffic court, teaching traffic classes and dealing with traffic tickets. There are millions of dollars being generated through the traffic courts, and the courts were filled every morning with violators with high penalty fees and court costs. Family court financially eclipses that by an incredibly wide margin. Back in the fifties and sixties, marriage was as permanent as tattoos. People got married, and that was it, no separating, no leaving, and no leaving the children behind. Of course, people had problems back then, but it wasn't socially acceptable for a husband to leave his wife and children. Back then, divorced women would scramble to find ways to keep their families afloat. Women didn't have the opportunity to get jobs that matched the men's income; therefore, they were always at the mercy of men to make money or bring home the bacon so to speak. Today, that's not the case; women can do anything a man can do, including leave an unhappy marriage. Move out with the kids, dissolve the marriage, get a settlement, and even get the spouse's name removed from the home they shared. And that's it, done deal, that part of their lives is over. Except, there's a child left behind, split between the two and forced to choose which one of the parents they would rather live with. That's a tough choice for a child, do they choose mommy and never see daddy again? Or choose daddy and break mommy's heart? After comprehending that mommy and daddy don't love each other anymore, a child may be left to believe that they're the cause of it all. They put unnecessary pressure on themselves and start blaming themselves for their parent's unsuccessful marriage. 85-90% of the time, they stay with the mother, and the father is held to financial responsibility. Immature men will abandon the relationship and throw the baby out with the dirty bathwater; in other words, they would discard the family while disposing of the relationship. He'd rather be absent than deal with the pain of a broken heart, which is throwing the responsibility of caring for his child out with the failed marriage. It is his ultimate choice to make sure to continue raising his kid even though the new limits to his involvement. Even on the other end, if the father was awarded custody. A small percentage of women would abandon the child regardless of the stigma it held. They would pursue unfulfilled dreams, other relationships, or employment. At times it could be for the sheer need to rediscover herself.

There are infinite scenarios that we can conclude how children are or feel like they are abandoned. Children will demonstrate behaviors and experience emotions aligned with abandonment no matter the reason. Divorce is drawn on a different canvas. The war between spouses leave children on the legal battlefield, and when all the inconsequential smoke clears, it's the children left to deal with the emotional carnage. It's easy when couples without children break up. It's a relatively clean break. They take what they came with, lick their wounds, and go their separate ways. Anything accrued together will be divided or voluntarily surrendered. What if one of the things acquired was a living being?

Let's say a pet. Adding a pet dog to the break-up equation complicates things. Who gets to keep the dog? The person who cared for it more? The one who walked it every morning? Do they call the dog into the room and see who it goes to first? Maybe, whoever paid for the majority of the food and vet bills? Or is it who spent the most time with the pet? All those questions usually get real sticky for couples trying to call it quits. Does one spouse want to keep the dog because they don't want the other to have it? Or does one partner want to be paid for half of the value and corresponding expenses paid out for the dog? Let's subtract the pet dog and factor in a child. Now, who gets the child? Do we use the same criteria as we do with property? Children may feel like pawns and pieces of property when parents use them for leverage. How do the courts know when parents are using children instead of truly putting the best interest of the children ahead of the money?

Is it the hurt feelings or injured egos? This reminds me of a story in 1st Kings of the Bible. In short, King Solomon had to resolve a dispute between two mothers on a baby and who the baby belonged to. The King couldn't possibly know who the baby boy belonged to, so he presented them with a solution. He ordered his men to cut the baby in half so both mothers could have equal parts of him. As the solider grabbed the baby and drew his sword, one of the women cried out and with great sorrow saying that the other woman can have the baby. The King then knew the woman that would give up the baby to save the baby's life must be the real mother. I wonder if divorcing parents would give up their desires in order to save their child's life? When the courts ask the sides to mediate, they're asking them to handle it before they come to court, or else the magistrate will do it for them. Usually, the question becomes, where does the child go? With the mom or with the dad? Do they use the same arguments for the child as they did for the family pet? Each case is individually unique, but in the majority of these cases, children are left with the mother. The father's are left with the financial support. For the fathers that leave the court feeling defeated may never pay child support or limit their support by hiding their income and assets. They consider child support payments as a punishment to them and an award to the mother. Some fathers may walk out of the court while simultaneously walking out for their child's life. This is a warped way of thinking, and the one it hurts most is the child. The mother will recover from his absence, but the child never will.

When spouses become co-parents, they have to endure the other spouse and any new romantic relationship that they may have formed out of their dissolution. Although emotionally difficult for the couple, it must be done for the sake of the children. This sounds like a no-brainer, but in many cases, it is not. Men will walk out of the marriage and out of their children's lives like it never happened. Abandoning the house, the marriage, the responsibilities, and most importantly, the children. The children did nothing wrong to deserve it, but are forced to accept his absence. When a father divorces his wife, the children feel divorced as well. This impacts them greatly. Depending on the circumstances behind the break-up, the children's emotional reaction can play out in several ways. For instance, if the couples were constantly fighting and creating a turbulent environment for the entire family. The children may feel a sigh of relief that he's gone, but will still exhibit abandonment traits because of his absence. On the other hand, if the family was happily intact, as far as the children knew, and then the parents abruptly decide to break up. The child may feel as though they were the reason for their parent's separation. They will rationalize it in ways to where they would harbor all the blame and begin to feel guilty. During this time of adjusting to their parents' separation and their father's distancing, they will feel a substantial degree of emotional isolation. The Father's absence influences the children's behavior, no matter how it happens. That's what marriage was initially meant for; it was designed for the children, not the parents. Lovers no longer choose a mate for childbearing but for superficial desires and if anything gets in the way of that. They break up, leaving the child with issues that will be with them for the rest of their lives.

Marriage is a union between two people and their children. Is divorce a separation from your partner and your children as well? When couples decide to dissolve their union, the children are the most important part of why some marriages last longer than they would otherwise. The two parties know it's over, but for the sake of the children, they stay together. During this time of waiting for the kids to grow up or move out of the house, the couple's agreement to have a conscious uncoupling can be tricky. They begin to treat each other like roommates instead of lovers. Children can easily pick up on these changed behaviors, and this can be emotionally unsettling for them. Previous generations didn’t have the preference to divorce. They were pressured socially to remain together, but in today's society, if the marriage becomes too challenging, then divorce is their first option. What's the big deal? Why stay in an unhappy, unfulfilling relationship? Some would say, why get married in the first place? For love? For security? Time or age? Children? Most will do it to have children. They would marry before they carry. In times before, it wasn't socially acceptable to have children before marrying, so people would rush to marry in order to have children. This usually wasn't the ideal foundation for a healthy, successful marriage, but it would satisfy the community, elders, and extended family. Couples that have children without nuptials, the children are considered to be born out of wedlock. The child, by definition, would be considered a bastard. It sounds harsh to refer to an innocent child as illegitimate, but that is the definition of it. Today there are millions of bastard children procreating in the same way. The value of marriage has diminished, while the number of childbirths has increased. The main cause of single-parent families is not only the high rates of divorce but the non-marital rates in childbearing. Couples feel it's much easier to leave a failing relationship than to leave a failing marriage. Non-committal relationships are the main culprit of unplanned pregnancies and thusly fatherless homes.

Marriage, like diamonds, should last forever, at least that's what the vows promise. Unfortunately, we know that nothing lasts forever, besides God's eternal love. As human beings, we change. Variations in our circumstances change, and feelings fade. For couples that marry young, they judge each other based on what their wants and needs are at the ages of 20-21. At ages 30-31, there's huge inequity between their two mating values on the mating market. If divorce happens, it's precisely because that which started as equitable mating values turned out to have a huge divergence on the mating market. That can put a strain on the marriage, especially if the wife's status goes up and his decline. Outside of marrying young, people just aren't willing to stay together if love, respect, and overall happiness doesn't exist. Some divorcees would agree that divorce can be more draining than their actual marriage, but in the same breath, they would still choose the path of least resistance for themselves, which is divorce.

Admittedly, staying together would most benefit the children if the environment was repairable and not toxic to the children. Couples will agree to separate and work on cleaning up their children's emotional mess later. And there will be a mess. Children in the middle of divorce are often beset by feelings of confusion, anxiety, and depression. In the past, individuals would throw divorce parties to celebrate the severance of their union. They take slices out of divorce cakes with "I Do Not," "Newly Unwed," or "To Your Happy Ending" written in icing. Comical sediment, but coming from a not so comical place. When exes glorify the severance of marriage, it speaks to only them, not to the children and the effects it's going to have on them. I'm all for happiness and couples concluding that the marriage didn't work, but to celebrate it, is unknowingly throwing it in the face of the blessings that came out of that union. The children. It's quoted in many Christian wedding ceremonies, "What God puts together, let no man break apart." This falls on deaf ears when your audience are children from previously broken families. To me, the only cases qualified for divorce are abuse and infidelity. If either party tolerates the marriage solely for money or status, that's the individual's decision. Do not involve the children in the battles of the relationship. It'll only subject them to more psychological pain in the long run. Once the marriage is consummated and kids are born, the couple can no longer make decisions individually, but collectively for the good of the children. That's why it's essential to make a sound decision to marry and have children. It shouldn't be a decision based out of fear, family pressure, or finance. Do people grow apart? Sure, they do, but as parents and partners, they should grow with each other, not from each other. To bring a child in the mix of a fear-based decision falls solely on that parents. Those selfish decisions will linger much longer than the person or persons who made them. It lives on in the next generation, that's what's wrong with the youth today? They are the results of the generation before them. The truth of the matter is, there are a lot of fathers that are less involved in family post-divorce. Naturally, the child will cling to their mother, and the father will experience less quality time with the child than the mother. That shouldn't deter a father from taking every opportunity to see his children. There's no good reason for abandonment.

Divorce for a child is a scar that takes an immense amount of time to heal. Don't assume the children will be okay. There will be emotional and psychological residue revealing itself in time through their behavior. Case in point with my next case study from the group. DEBBIE DIVORCE, a true rocker girl. She's in her early twenties with shoulder-length hair and one side shaved, and the other side dyed purple. She didn't wear much makeup, but she always had smoky eyes and dark eyeliner. The first time I saw her, she had a red plaid shirt wrapped around her waist, ripped black jeans, and a black tee that read, "I SPEAK FOUR LANGUAGES-

English, Profanity, Sarcasm and Shit." She always had in-ear headphones attached to her phone, so it was hard to gauge if she was listening or not. Learning more about her, Debbie came from a family that was upper middle class and lives a privileged life and operates non-apologetic about it. Her parents divorced when she was thirteen, and she ricocheted in and out of trouble ever since. Studies show that adolescents are the most affected when it comes to coping with their parent's divorce. Younger children may not remember that parents' divorce, while young adult children will be more likely to accept that their parents are no longer together. The children between the ages of 13-19 are the ones that struggle most with the adjustment, generally having problems expressing their feelings, turning away from family, and choosing to deal with their emotions on their own. Debbie Divorce is no different. After her parents' divorce, she closed up and didn't trust anyone with her feelings. She reveals that her parents were great friends to each other, but terrible parents to her. During the marriage, her father was always away on business trips, and he rarely called home. It was always a treat when he did phone home. The times he was home, he'd keep busy by finding new fix-it projects around the house that needed tending to, hence not allowing any free time to play with her. At times, she felt as though she was bothering him, and over time she learned to leave him alone and just play with her toys. Debbie grew up with both parents, but in retrospect, she was emotionally abandoned by her father. The divorce was par for the course for her; there were no over's or under's. She broke even when it came to seeing her father. Over time she saw him less to eventually not seeing him at all for many years. That emotional abandonment she felt has now morphed into a physical abandonment. In our sessions, her voice began to crack when she got to the end of her story,

DEBBIE DIVORCE - I remember asking my mother, why did he leave? Was it me? I believed he loved me but didn't like me.

Counselor Danita did her best to reassure Debbie that it was not her, but children who are adjusting to divorce often feel guilty and blame themselves for breaking up the family. Most become depressed because they felt rejection from their fathers. Their self-esteem drops, and they may withdraw from certain activities that they use to enjoy. Children from divorce presuppose that things don't last forever because their parent decides to call it quits. I can't imagine the children's feelings when someone that important walks out of their lives—the deep wound of insecurity and distrust leaves. Nine times out of ten, they'll have difficulties in their relationships and more likely get divorced themselves. For Debbie, she believes this to be true in totality, because now as an adult, she has it engrained in her head that she wasn't enough to keep her parents together and mirror that same "not enough" disposition into her relationships. She dated qualified boyfriends in the past but seemed to always find some misdemeanor offense with them to break up. She became grossly introverted and gradually shut out the trusted ones around her. She began reading dark novels, listening to dark music, wearing dark clothing, and reflected dark emotions at times. She soon went in and out of a state of depression, speaking less, and becoming more of a recluse.

Debbie Divorce wasn't always the rocker goth girl. She says she was considered the quintessential mild-mannered fun, happy, outgoing, good girl by her friends and schoolmates. Some of her childhood friends were surprised to see her years later dressed in the garb we see her in today. She recognizes that the genesis of her darkness started a bit after the divorce of her parents. She further states that she was formerly engaged to marry a great guy, her knight in shining armor, her prince charming. According to her, he was handsome, loving, had a great career, and came from a great family with both parents who were married for over 30 years. She made it a point to add that last part, which tells me that the guy's parents' relationship intimidated her. Long story short, things didn't work out because deep down inside, she couldn't trust that a loving relationship could last. Despite his promise to marry, she still had doubts and trust issues within herself. Her heart was filled with lingering doubts about the true meaning of unconditional love. Her strongest example of an attempt was her very own parents, and they fell short of it. Debbie's thinking was, she had no chance at it at all, so why try? The poor guy had no power over her decision to call it off. It was nothing he could do to change her mind because the change had to come from inside her. He was powerless and heartbroken. From her words, she was certain it was because of what she witnessed her parents went through in their divorce. She feared the same fate and projected that into her relationship. She felt as though she was better off being alone than being hurt from an invested relationship with nothing to show for it in the end. In times of divorce for children, they need to feel included and aware of the love each parent feels for them. They cannot feel like it's their fault or that they were the reasons for any conflict. Although Debbie's parents reassured her that it wasn't her fault, she still felt differently because her father never came back around to see her. Video calls turned into phone calls, which turned into no calls at all. On her birthday, she says she may or may not get a card. She remembers one card she did receive read, 'Get your gift from the alimony I paid your mother.' How cruel to take a jab at her mother through a birthday wish for his daughter. She always felt divorced from her father too.

According to many psychological studies, children from divorced families have a wide array of emerging problems. Incidents of behavioral and learning disorders are revealed due to the lack of having that father's presence, his discipline, and his guidance during key developmental stages in their lives. Physical effects can set in like headaches, speech impediments, and asthma, yes, asthma. Emotional effects can be overwhelming, and children from divorced families are twice as likely to attempt suicide than children in a two-parent household. It also affects them sociologically; not having a father around can limit their educational resources compared to their peers, not from divorced homes. It gives them a higher dropout rate. The effects on children of divorce are not too different from the physical, emotional, and sociological effects children from abandonment have. For the children not living with their fathers, 40% of them won't even see him for a year due to relocation and may not visit his home at all within that year.

One can only imagine that if those effects overlay each other, it could double the likeliness and make it more difficult for a child to avoid. Spouses become co-parents, and children become statistics. After the divorce and all the dust settles, it's children like Debbie who are left to pick up the pieces. 25% of them will witness the breakup of a parent's second marriage, and 10% will see a third and fourth subsequent marital breakup. The hope for success in their relationships gets more frightening as they watch their parents re-start love over and over again.

Even though I'm highlighting the negative aspects of divorce, I also believe that it is important to note that in cases of domestic violence, abuse, or any other harmful behavioral patterns on the part of one or both parents, divorce can be the only answer to ensure the psychological safety of the children. Some parents that are reluctant to divorce each other solely for the sake of the children but are destructive to each other can do more harm than good to their kids. As a parent, you will know that children are like sponges, absorbing information around them as quickly as possible, consciously or subconsciously. The child will pick up on his/her parents slowly growing apart. They're shifts in behavior; now, an occasional dispute will result in hostility towards one another. At times, the children will get caught up in their parents' tug of war and find themselves standing in as referees to their parent's disagreements, thus giving them the impression that they can resolve their parent's problems when they cannot. They blame themselves, and this is where guilt sets in.

Furthermore, the root of indecision for these adults lies in an early-childhood parental divorce. When a child thinks that he or she has to make a decision between the parents and to choose who's right and who's wrong, this will resonate with a child not only in the short term but over a long-term period. They'll always question themselves on the decisions they were forced to make in those times.

Failing marriages that contain children are complicated. When a spouse feels trapped in an un-thriving marriage, this can affect the children, and they can be exposed to derogating behavior. Unknowingly or knowingly, the disputing parents can begin to take their marital frustrations out on the child. In this case, I'm in total support of the dissolution of their union to spare the child of long-term emotional pains. In all other instances, I'm on the side of resolution and working it out. Where there was once love, there can be hope. Some spouses will stay together because they're afraid of change. Religious reasons or simply because one spouse won't let go. To stay together solely for the children can be problematic, not just for the squabbling couple, but for the children. I usually pose why and how questions to couples that want to get a divorce. HOW did it get to this? And WHY is divorce the only resolution? After that, I'd follow it up with, WHAT changed? And WHEN did this change take place? Lastly, I'd ask, did that change change the person or the situation? These questions aren't hard to answer, but it opens up the minds and gives voice to the core of the real issues. When I ask about the children, it's usually, "They'll be fine." The truth is, no, they won't. They will get through it, but it will have lasting effects on them. If for nothing else, it'll affect their ability to resolve relationships. For children that observe parents in dispute, it's not a far reach to understand why 44% of children's first marriage ends up in a divorce. Parents fight in front of their children all the time but resolve their problems behind closed doors. That's not healthy to teach a child. They need to see and hear their parent's make-up as well. If they only witness the fighting but never see the resolution, it can be confusing to their development when things simply go back to normal.

In a "Me Society," it's all about my happiness right now, and if I'm not happy, I can't make my kids happy. If that's the case, ask the children what would make them happy. Most answers would be for their parents to love each other and stay together as a family. But it's not about the child's happiness. It's about the divorcing parents and what makes them happy. When I listen to couples give the reasons for divorce, the feeling is truly sincere, but the grounds upon which they began to feel that way were fixable. Usually, couples want to blame each other and take none of the blame themselves. I listen, but I want to know more about the individual and what changed within them in the marriage? Does the decision you made at the time of marriage still line up with the decision you're making at the time of the divorce? Most of the time, it doesn't. When the true reasons why couples get married are exposed, the decision made was never about the other person's happiness. It was about their own. When the moment that happiness is threatened, the marriage will be in jeopardy. All these things are not the problem of the child. They didn't have a say in their parents' choice of partnership. All they know is that the two people before them should love each other equally as they love them. As the child gets older, he/she will understand that some things don't last forever, but to be introduced to it in the early stages of development can cause many long-term effects. Those effects will vary between age and circumstances. Infants up to two years old may be too young to be affected initially, but the effects of seven to twelve-year-old, like in Debbie Divorces' case, will display some distrust to their parents. They'll start having problems in school, and their social behavior will take a noticeable shift.

Teens will have the worst time adjusting to the change. They may turn away from their family entirely and find other ways to cope with their parents' divorce. They may periodically lash out at the custodial parent for the separation and ignore the other parent for leaving. Teens can become very ashamed of their parents' divorce. It damages their self-esteem and confidence. It's a hard time for the children of all ages. They may display clinging behavior or withdraw; they can become hostile at school or with friends, or even act out sexually. That's why it's vitally important that the needs of the children be balanced against the needs of the parents. The child should keep in touch with both parents and retain a healthy relationship with both. What's disturbing to me is when some scorned mothers use their children to retaliate against the father. This doesn't only hurt the man, but it damages the child because we now know that separation from the father will negatively impact their lives. Mothers that badmouth and counter previous disciplines established by the father only exacerbates an already traumatic and upsetting situation. Keeping a child from his father is a cruel and heinous act and should never be the remedy of a dispute between spouses. Dealing with a divorce is already hard enough to force a father's absence into the equation, only compounds an inescapable emotional pain for the child. There's no guarantee that after a divorce, a father's influence will change the behaviors of a child, but him remaining a constant figure in their lives would make their transition much smoother.

There are so many emotions going through all the parties involved, and the fathers themselves aren't exempt from the effects of a failed marriage. They also feel hurt and pain of failure. When men no longer feel useful in a relationship, they begin to deteriorate from the inside out. Emotional problems quickly turn into communication problems, and when the communication breaks down, so does the marriage. Feelings of depression, bewilderment, loss, and anxiety all keep company with divorce for men. He fears that he'll become a visitor in his child's life, rather than being that daily stabilizing influence like he has been during the marriage.

Consequently, for the child, the routine is their reliable resource of reassurance, so when this is taken away, the father-child relationship slowly deteriorates. Their feeling of security and certainty has been threatened, and one by one, layer by layer, emotional bricks begin to stack, constructing their walls of defense. As they enter adulthood, they begin to fear rejection and have little to no trust in their now-adult relationships. If their fathers abandoned them during the divorce process, it's empirical that they acknowledge the truth of their injuries and change the way they think about themselves. This strengthens mental and emotional health and welcomes in growth. For parents that are getting divorced, they should pay less attention to who gets what in the settlement and more attention to the emotional needs of their children. Without these things in place, the children are likely to repeat the same patterns of their parents for generations to come. I advise couples to choose wisely, not hastily, because being a single parent has a substantial degree of emotional isolation and an unsettling effect on a child's social and emotional development. When fantasy doesn't meet reality in marriage, couples are quick to call it quits. The only one that can't quit on the family is the child. They're bound by blood between the two disputing parental parties. It is important to understand that children have a sense of loyalty to each parent and feel like they're betraying one parent or another when that loyalty is threatened. Children of divorce need to be spared the antagonistic feelings of their parents and not put in the middle of their battles. In such an atmosphere, it is more difficult for children to flourish. Mental health issues and behavioral problems are a direct result of an environment created by the injured parents. Hurt in the relationship or hurt in their very own upbringing. Parents that were hurt or injured by their parent's divorce or their father's abandonment don't realize that they are repeating a dilapidating cycle with their children.

Despite popular belief, fathers fight for custody of their children all the time, not in terms of ownership of the children, but in terms of residence. They want the children to live with them so that they won't lose that bond, but in very few cases will the father be granted full custody. For men, there's a sense of fear of losing their children when divorce is mentioned. Although a stable home, parenting abilities, and financial strengths are weighed, in most cases, mothers are given preference. As the quote goes, "Happy wife, happy life." If the mother isn't happy, then how can she raise her kids in a healthy environment? Which, to her, is more emotionally detrimental to her children than not having their father around. Outside of abuse or an arranged marriage, sometimes the decision for divorce is minimal and can be resolved with some counseling. When marriages run into problems of finance, it weighs heavy on the men. For most men, they must be the provider, and if they can't provide, they feel inadequate and unworthy. If this happens, communication becomes laborious at best, which can break the emotional and sexual connection. Chances are signs of physical, mental, or emotional abuse that will follow, which should be unacceptable and divorce worthy for either gender.

If we are totally honest, most divorces are motivated by the fact that women will more than likely be awarded the children, the house, and the money. Court records reflect this fact and have shown that women initiate three-quarters of divorces, and 89% of the cases end with the custody being awarded to the mother. Now, we probably all know of people who've married for money, power, prestige, or name recognition. Both men and women. Marriage for women requires three basic needs; Love, security, and safety. They want to know that you *love* them, that you won't *leave* them, and that you won't *hurt* them. If any of those are breached, the heart voids out the trust she had in him, and the bond begins to fracture. If infidelity was the culprit, then the trust vacates immediately, and it'll take time to build it back up.

A person should not have to tolerate bad behavior in their relationship. Once the respect goes out the door, then so should you. To remain in a contemptuous relationship isn't healthy, but to marry into one is insane. When a person willingly enters into a relationship with a partner with significant red flags, it's only delaying the inevitable. Ignored red flags are a delayed dissolution waiting to happen. I'm not recommending you to leave the relationship immediately. I'm only asking that those potential problems be addressed. The alternative of jumping from one relationship to another is only practicing divorce. Being accustomed to loving and leaving over and over again will soon become an ongoing pattern that won't be so easy to break.

I suggest to grow up and stop playing house and start paying attention to yourself. Learn yourself, your likes and dislikes, your wants and needs, your love languages, and take your time in finding the person that understands and mirrors those same qualities. Sadly, we have to revert to relationship class 101 to avoid bringing a child into an unstable situation that will undoubtedly damage them if the relationship dissolves. You'll do yourself a great service by evaluating your partner thoroughly with an honest and truthful measuring stick that's not swayed by money, status, religion, family, or social pressures. I'm a strong believer in the once upon a time and happily ever after. Still, I'm also a big advocate of sitting down with marriage counselors, therapists and/or a religious entity before hiring a divorce lawyer. Today's divorcees are more concerned with their immediate personal happiness than working towards better long-established happiness that will benefit them and the children involved. I can hear people now yelling at these pages, "I tried!" and "You don't know my situation." I hear those people, and I understand that often the hardest part of the escape is the decision to make it. At the end of the day, every situation is unique and has its own storyline. Still, one thing is for sure; the child will be emotionally affected regardless of the circumstances behind the separation. Those are the facts because young children can't decipher the understandings between adults. They listen to their parents explain why mommy and daddy can't live together anymore, but that won't lessen the pain. It takes two to make it work, and if both parties aren't willing to take a real valiant effort on patching the marriage back together, not for the kids, but for themselves, then things won't get better, and the talks of divorce will be eminent. It's sad but true that the courts are filled to the brim with these dissolution cases. There are many reasons for seeking advice for divorce. Toxic relationships, arranged marriages, adultery, or abuse (physical, mental, or emotional), to name a few. But the fact of the matter is that both parties are responsible for their actions, and what can't be solved in the house must be solved out of the house with counseling. A qualified third party listening and administrating devices to save the marriage may help a couple returning to the trust and love they shared. Recurrently, the children are the only innocent bystanders left watching the adhesive of their family bond be ripped apart. Whether you side with reconciliation or termination of the relationship, one thing is certain; a father's presence is important to a child's development and is damaging in his absence.

Substitute Fathers

In 2019, U.S. President Donald Trump had quickly undone policies that protected many undocumented immigrants from deportation. A father was deported after living 40 years in the U.S., leaving his wife financially burdened and his children abandoned. This have had devastating impacts on many children of deported parents. When a family unit is broken, a surge of long term emotional and physical ailments begin to set in. Depression, anger, resentment or anxieties all can lead to drug and alcohol abuse, criminal behavior, sexual deviancy, and at the very worse, suicide. The U.S. needs to find a better way to consider the strength of an immigrant's connections to the United States before deciding whether they should be deported or not. My concern is, all while lawmakers and administration figures out how to best strategize the immigration reform, the children are left without a father. That missing piece will have lasting effects that will shape them as adults. As human beings, why aren't we giving them the best opportunity to succeed? The U.S. has forced abandonment upon American born children. Will the U.S. now foster those children and become their substitute parents? I've heard too many horror stories about foster care and almost an equal amount about substitute fathers, who were emotionless, abusive, or perverted. They had no paternal blood connection to the children. The substitute father, which is the replacement of the absent father, makes me think about lions in the wild. When a male lion challenges another male lion with his pride of lioness and cubs, it's dangerous for the entire pride. Because if the challenger wins, he will kill the cubs to end the bloodline of the defeated king, then proceed to mate with all of the lioness to have cubs of his own. It's a horrible circle of life, and to the cubs, the substitute father can be a threat to their delicate and vulnerable lives.

Not all substitute fathers are men looking to eliminate another man's bloodline, but some can be careless, and it can trickle down from a fatherless adult to a fatherless child. Meet Diego; we'll call him STEP DAD DIEGO. He joined the group early one Saturday morning. He was mandated by the court to take DUI classes, Anger Management classes, and also attend AA meetings. He lost his license due to his third Driving Under the Influence charge (DUI). He was assigned to another class across town, but being that he was using public transportation, it was too far to travel for him. This chapter highlights how being raised by a substitute father; although it is a blessing for the child, it can also be their worst nightmare.

Diego couldn't drive because he would jeopardize his freedom with mandatory incarceration and tons of fines. Lucky for him, he found this class within walking distance from the bus stop. Step Dad Diego, like many other people in the class, was not happy about attending group every week. The difference with Diego, he let everyone know his disdain for his being there. The coffee was always too cold or the doughnuts too stale, the room too stuffy, his chair too lumpy. He'd complain about everything from the lights being too bright, to the air quality being too low. He'd use any excuse to disturb the session. This one particular day, while everyone was reflecting on their weekend, Diego yells out in Spanish, "Can you please hurry up, your voice is annoying." No one understood him and chalked it up as Diego being disgruntled

Diego. Counselor Danita fired back, not in her usual soft, soothing voice, but with a more direct, authoritative tone, "There's no reason to be rude, Mr. Hernandez, just say what's on your mind." then in Spanish, she asks, "Would you like to share with the group? If not, please apologize, and we can get started." Diego takes a beat, surprised that she understood and spoke Spanish. He sank deep into his seat, and humbly responded in English. "Excuse me, please." Everyone was impressed, and I believe that that moment established new-found respect for Counselor Danita.

Step Dad Diego tells his story of physical and verbal abuse from his biological father before he abandoned the family, then sexually abused by his step-father. He lost all trust in men early on in his life. That was the moment he placed his first couple of bricks on his defensive wall. Everyone has a wall they've built up as a barrier between anything that'll harm them emotionally. Usually, it's used in terms of intimacy, but Diego uses it to protect himself from the truth of his molestation. He builds his wall high in order to hide his secret. We all appreciated Diego openly removing one brick from his wall to allow us to hear his story. His father, whom he knew up until the time he was five, suddenly leaves never to return, causing mistrust, which is a pivotal component in abandonment issues. As I sat through this dialogue between them, I understood that there were multiple emotional layers to people from fatherless homes.

We began to peel back more as the session continued. One thing that Diego did do was take full responsibility for his actions. We add a brick that blocks and remove a brick that frees you. The acceptance of his responsibility is a freeing brick. Unfortunately, it's a blocking brick that doesn't forgive. The more bricks you have, the taller the wall and more difficult for others to come in or, more importantly, get out. That's trust. Diego and people like him don't trust easily or at all at times. I believe the walls they've constructed is not only to keep people out but for them to be safely behind. Diego's father was abandoning the relationship, and subsequently, he and his siblings have created the foundation for his wall. The minute he begins to remove those trust and unforgiving bricks, he'll begin to heal from the inside. The anger will dissipate, and the trust will return. It was freeing him from anxiety and any signs of resentment.

Counselor Danita put it in a way that a five-year-old could understand. Ultimately, everyone has bricks to remove, whether it's bricks of trust, intimacy, unforgiveness, hate, resentment, anger, etc. We all need to recognize our bricks and remove them from our defensive walls—one brick at a time. It shouldn't be determined by someone else. Do not allow one person or one event to define who you are. There are many layers to you that need to be unraveled, but you can't even begin to peel back those layers if you're stuck in the past. That creates a fortress of bricks that surrounds you and keeps you trapped in. Sitting in these sessions has taught me how valuable counseling is to the community. These things that people are discovering about themselves will catapult them into a place they've never been, a place of freedom from their past. Thinking that that was all we needed to hear from Diego, Counselor Danita uncovered another layer with him. After a smoke break, she began again on Diego.

COUNSELOR - After the abuse from your step-father, did your mother leave him?

STEP DAD DIEGO - No, she didn't want to believe it was true. As soon as I was old enough, I moved out. I don't trust my mother to protect me from him if he wanted to touch me again.

COUNSELOR - Did he?

STEP DAD DIEGO - No, I never brought it up again. I let it go and buried that "brick" a long time ago, and I don't want to dig it back up. What I did do was stop listening to both of them. I didn't care anything about following rules or their wishes. I did my own thing. I called my step-father, the substitute. You know how you can get away with mischief at school with a sub, but not your teacher?

The room nodded in agreeance.

STEP DAD DIEGO - That's what I was doing. I was getting into trouble all the time. Not coming home after school, getting into all types of shit in my neighborhood.

COUNSELOR - Do you blame yourself for your father not coming back into your life?

STEP DAD DIEGO - I did at first because I was a bad vato. Ya know.

COUNSELOR - Diego, your father left because he wanted to leave, and you had no part in it. He chose to leave. You or your mother couldn't make him stay. It's in his personality and his imprint that he abandons the family. There was nothing you could do to stop it. Stop blaming yourself and remove that brick of blame from your wall.

It was obvious that being molested as a child has changed him, but being molested by his step-father made him. I guess I shouldn't be too dumbfounded by his story, being that 20% of fatherless children are molested by someone close to them. I've summed up Diego's session with the fact that some of his issues come from being abandoned as a child. He harbors emotions that have seeped into his adult life and caused troubles for him. His father was an alcoholic, and now he's dealing with those same issues to cope with or cover up deeper problems he doesn't want to address, the molestation. His step-father abused him early on shortly after finding out his real father was never returning. He latched onto another father figure and trusted him, and unfortunately, his trust was met with molestation. Adult retrospective studies from the Center for Disease Control and Prevention in 2006 shows that 1 in 4 women and 1 in 6 men were sexually abused before the age of 18. That's more than 43 million adult survivors of child sexual abuse in the U.S.; 73% of child victims do not tell anyone about the abuse for at least a year. 45% of victims do not tell anyone for at least five years. Some never disclose the act at all. Family structure is the most important risk factor in child sexual abuse. Children who live with two married biological parents are at a lower risk for abuse—the risk increases when children live with step-parents or a single parent. Children living without either parent (foster children) are ten times more likely to be sexually abused than children that live with both biological parents. Children who live with a single parent that has a live-in partner are at the highest risk: they are 20 times more likely to be victims of child sexual abuse than children living with both biological parents.

Diego's problems started when his father left, but it worsened when his substitute father, cloaked in step-dad clothing, moved in. The reason I started this chapter off with the separation of fathers from their children and told the story of how that affected Diego was to demonstrate how no matter the circumstances leading to a child being separated from their fathers, it will affect them. Abandon children can attach themselves to another father figure that enters their lives. We must be careful to whom that figure is because molesters come in all shapes and sizes. The actions of a predator comes from a selfish sexual intent. It's a momentary satisfaction to fulfill their sexual controlling fantasies. Momentary for them, but leaves a lasting stigma of mental and emotional anguish for the abused.

See often, where there's one person in a position of power such as a parent, a pastor, a priest, a coach, a teacher, or a close relative, it gives children the allusion that it's safe to listen to their every instruction. Most sexual abusers are respected members of the community and are not privy to any particular age group, race, or religion. Not questioning if it's the right or wrong thing to do, they assume it must be right because it's coming from an adult. Molesters groom their victims to gain trust, power, and control, and once they've achieved that, they shame their victims into not sharing this terrible secret. For those who were abused as children may understand better about keeping "it" a secret. Victims live with this veil of shame throughout their abuse and it can last for the rest of their lives, if they let it. The shame that they experience feels real, and it cannot be discounted, but in actuality, it's only an illusion set forth by their abuser to maintain control. The primary experience of a victim is fear and betrayal. Fear of not pleasing the person of power or fear of physical harm to oneself or harm of loved ones around. The secondary experience is the earlier in childhood the abuse happens, the more negatively the impact will have. It'll alter the development of the brain, especially the right brain, which regulates emotion, which later in their lives could lead to a predisposition to the use of drugs or alcohol abuse and possibly sexual abuse to others. Yes, when children are sexually abused by an adult, it can often lead them into acting out those same abuses on other children.

Parents have to be more vigilant with monitoring their children, although sexual predators can fool even the parents. I can't blame parents for the acts of others, but imagine the children without the protection and guidance of a father? They're left to fend for themselves, and as a child, they lack the coping skills of adults, so when they become adults, they chalk it up as something they've always dealt with. They normalize it and simply say, "That's just the way I am." which is far from the truth. It's not who you are or what you are, you were abused, and you need to deal with it to become who you really are. We, as adults, carry sins done to us from our childhood into our adulthood, and it begins to shape us as people. When all we have to do is recognize the abuse and the abuser, forgive them and yourself, and move on. Don't carry it any longer; leave that brick on the ground. The adults that are acting un adult-like are the violators, and they are the ones who are disturbed. Do not treat others as if they were the ones who hurt you, because they smell like, look like, or speak like your abuser.

Stop giving a molester power over you in the form of hate and unforgiveness. Let it go and recognize that they're the ones with the problem, not you, even if it's your immediate family members. Give them no more power. Confront them and leave it there. Stop demanding an apology or needing them to take responsibility for their actions; they won't do it. They'll act like it never happened. Then you should state it loud and firm on what they did every time they want to talk to you. Remind them of what they did. They don't have the right to speak to you unless it comes on your terms and with full accountability. Eventually, they'll stop pretending, and you can move forward in strength. A molester grooms their victims to gain trust, power, and control. You must take your power back. I've given one example, but they're many ways to achieve your strength, and you need to find yours. Do not allow what they've done to you yesterday to seep into your today's life. Their horrendous acts should no longer victimize your today's relationships or your today's lifestyle and friendships. Some victims of molestation can be turned off to sexual intercourse entirely, or get turned on to the opposite sex to avoid anything that resembles their abuser. If, at an early age, you were exposed to something sexually inappropriate, it may have skewed your development sexually and activated a part of you that wasn't ready for intimacy. This can confuse a child or pre-teen. This can carry over into your adulthood if never confronted and put to rest.

Diego did not want to talk about the molestation his step-father committed on him. Most men are embarrassed to speak about any sexual abuse and keep the abuse bottled up inside until it bubbles into hate, anger and/or abuse to others. In his case, he's abused himself. Many children who were sexually abused early in life develop what psychologists call “Implicit Memories,” which are non-verbal memories. It could be a certain smell or look or place that brings them back to the abuse and cause them to react in a defense or avoidance type of way. What I've found in my 20 plus years of working with teens, pre-teens, and young adults, is that even those who can identify key moments of their abuse typically do not have a fraction of awareness of how pervasive and far-reaching into their adult life that abuse can go. For example, someone can be molested, but may not know it at the point of it's happening. Something tells them that it doesn't feel right, but they trust the abuser and then feel ashamed that they didn't know any better. As the abused ages, they feel slightly different, a bit out casted, or damaged. It can cause the abused to either reframe from sex entirely or indulge in it insatiably. Some are so emotionally distraught that they avoid the gender of the abuser and turn to the same sex as a safe place partner. What they cannot tell you is that their dirty little secret has affected everything around them, from the way they chose their friendship circles, employment, education, relationships, and in some cases, even their religion. It affects how much confidence they have or lack thereof and, at the very least, what they require of themselves. What are they telling themselves, what's the dialogue? I'm not good enough, or I don't deserve to be with this person or that person, or who would ever want me? The things they tell themselves about themselves comes from an abused child's point of view. It was created at a point of the abuse and compounded like interest upon itself as long as the secret was kept. The event can never be changed, but the language you use about yourself can. I'm damaged, or feeling you're not worthy because of the internal dialogue you're having with yourself, and that needs to change. Sometimes what happens to us can happen for us. Turn your tragedy into triumph.

Adversity builds character; some of the most tragic, hurtful events cause people to rise from the ashes like a Phoenix. Oftentimes, they take their bad experiences and turn it around to create something of value. Take for instance, the child who grows up with an alcoholic parent, like Diego. They may decide to never have a drink out of fear in falling into that very same addiction or become more addicted themselves. Or the child that grows up in an abusive household and vows never to treat his counterpart in the same manner and claims victory over it. These adults recognized at a younger age that what they were witnessing was not the right thing to do and changed their behaviors. They were adamant in their choices and chose to recognize the problem and ignored the old saying, "Children do as I say and not as I do." Now it all doesn't fall on not having your father around because molestation can happen anytime and anywhere, but more often than not, children that come from fatherless homes rank pretty high as in Step Dad Diego's case. His father abandoned the family at an early age, and that left him feeling confused and lost. He tried so hard not to be like his biological father but subsequently became that same thing. He learned how not to obey authority at home and got into all kinds of trouble. His mother worked tireless hours, and in her absence, his step-father abused him. When it hits home for Diego, he wondered why his real father never came back to save him. He even pleaded with his mother to tell him the whereabouts of his father, only to find out that the truth was his real father simply and willfully abandoned him. That later led to his reckless behavior and heavy drinking, but it's not all Diego's fault, because sexual abuse changes people and their behaviors. Emotional deregulations can lead to addiction, depression, anxiety, problems with intimacy, problems with sexual dysfunction, problems with sexual orientation confusion, and an increased risk for suicide.

Although it was honorable for Diego's step-dad to step in and take on the role of the father, he took advantage of his authority and Diego's innocence when he sexually abused him. His step-father created a veil of shame for Diego. Even though this isolated event was a defining event in his life, it doesn't define him. He doesn't have to be invisible any longer. 90% of molesters target children they know. It's all about power and control, and once it's taken away from the victim, they're on an endless journey to get it back. In Diego's case, his power and control were taken away, so drinking and numbing the past was his version of taking back the control. If someone is hurting you, they're in control of what your body feels, but if you're hurting yourself, you feel that you have power and control over your own skin. Other kids abuse food by overeating or not eating enough, some by trying to please everyone (class clowns), some by being invisible and retreating into oneself while others become trouble makers or bullies. Their coping mechanism is to hurt others the way they were being hurt at home. Some kids become overachievers and OCD in their projects. These kids are very unforgiving of themselves if they're any less than perfect.

Many famous people aren't exempt from sexual abuse as children. Most victims immerse themselves in a hobby or their imagination to drown out said childhood abuse. Most are successful, and others are not, but all have some form of side effects such as anxiety, addiction, depression, and the most dangerous, suicide. When I decided to write this book on fatherless children and the effects it had on people as adults, I wanted to get a wide range of point of views and stories. As Obama left office after an eight-year two-term Presidency, President Trump stepped in and put a travel ban on certain countries. So, when I had the chance to travel to Cuba, I went. I took my pen and pad to document anyone that were raised without a father. Upon arrival, it was a apparent that the country had deep scars of civil destruction. A great deal of the buildings in Havana bore bullet holes and chunks of missing walls. Most of the people were hard working day laborers trying to rebuild their lives amidst the constant revolutionary reminders. It's been 30 years since U.S. citizens could travel there, and I took full advantage of it. My tour guide/translator helped me navigate through the city, sharing a wealth of his homelands history and culture. What he also shared was his story of his missing father. His father defected to Miami years ago and never returned. He was left looking from the war-ridden banks of Cuba across the ocean every day, wondering if he would ever see his father again. As we drove past the U.S. Embassy along the coastline of the forbidden city, he pointed across the waters towards Miami and flicked his cigar bud out of the window, "That's where my father is." He had a light hearted scoff, but I could tell there was pain in his words. We pulled up to the La Floridita Restaurant in Old Havana, a favorite place of the famous American author, Ernest Hemingway. Hemingway often sat at the end of the bar and wrote notes for his masterpieces. The bar even has a life-sized bronze statue of him in his favorite seat. As I spoke to people, I found out more about Hemingway, I discovered that he was sexually abused as a child and suffered depression because of it. He later committed suicide. I'm not sure of the direct correlation it has to his childhood abuse, but his father committed suicide as well. One thing for certain, it's no coincidence that adults that suffer from depression and attempts of suicide are the ones that have symptoms of some sexual, emotional, or physical abuse early in their childhood. Here's are statics on the effects of these abuses:

- 97% depression.
- 60% of sexual dysfunction (problems with intimacy, libido, orgasms, and impotence).
- 49% of Anxiety/Panic attacks or Phobias.
- 48% of suicide/suicide attempts (this is the most dangerous).
- 48% of substance abuse.
- 46% varies psychoses.

Other problems can include Dissociation, Borderline Personality Disorder (BPD), self-mutilation, Sexual Identity Disorder, Antisocial Personality. Most victims experience and display more than one of these symptoms. You never know what kids are going home to once they leave school, after school programs or practices. We believe they're going home to a safe, loving environment when at times, they may be going straight to the clutches of their abusers. During the Covid-19 pandemic in 2020, reports stated that child abuse rose substantially. Mental, physical and sexual. How do children relate to love when love ones abuse them? Specifically, children of molestation, they may never know how to love because they've never seen it. The ones they trusted were the ones that abused them under the cloak of love. Therefore, to express love to another may come with a lot of pain and confusion. Until they learn to stop giving their abuser power, they will continue to live in a confused state when it comes to love.

Let's not give all step-fathers a bad rap. There are plenty of men that have stepped up and stepped into a child's life and made tremendous differences. The situation that happened to Diego is an unfortunate one, and many victims live in a state of numbed detachment. They've learned how to bottle up their pain and keep it behind closed doors, well hidden from the public. Childhood abuse is kept secret for many adults, but sharing their stories gives voice to their physical symptoms. The anger, the trust issues, denial, the numbing (drugs, alcohol, self-mutilation, etc.), and the fear of the secret being exposed only allows the abuse to continue. Again, I am always amazed at how closely physical ailments can reflect trauma. Hopefully, this book will help connect the dots between what has happened to the abused and where they find themselves today. Remember, the information I'm sharing is designed for a broad audience and shouldn't be a replacement to seek a professional evaluation. I needed to add this disclaimer for my readers so that they continue to seek healing. If your child or any children you suspect are dealing with any of the previous mentioned symptoms, seek the assistance of a Clinical Psychologist. Or seek out legal help to prosecute those that abused you or your child.

Step Up Dads

A father is to a man as Van Gogh is to an aspiring artist; he's the blueprint. Fathers play an important role in a man's development or lack thereof. Men without fathers usually get their idea of what a man should be from outsiders, and these outside influences aren't always positive. Even men that mean well can still instill warped understandings of what real men should be. Universal statements like "Real men don't cry.", "A woman's place is in the kitchen.", or "Children are to be seen, not heard." can corrupt a young man's outlook on the world and, ultimately, how it views him. Without a father in a young man's life, he could be swayed by anything or anyone without the essence of what a real man is to be. He may be insecure in his ability to be a man and/or confused about what the role of a man is if he didn't have a father in his life. Without having an example of how a man should manage his emotions, children and young adults may morph into a type of man that ignores their feelings and has a hard time displaying them to others.

Step Up Dads are the men that have stepped into children's lives that aren't their own and positively changed their lives with unconditional love and guidance. The reason why I revere these men so much is because they have stepped in when others have stepped out. They give children great joy in knowing that they are worthy of love regardless of the actions of other men. This chapter resonates with my personal story because my biological father didn't raise me. I was too loved to know that the father raising me wasn't the father that made me. This was the most emotional and challenging chapter for me to write. Not because it required me to dig deep into my transparency about my biological father, but because during the composing of these pages, I loss the only man I ever knew as my father, my step-up dad, Mr. James Garrett, passed away. He knew exactly what he meant to me. I remember lying next to him on his hospital bed and expressing how proud I was to call him my father and how much I appreciated his unconditional love. He blindly loved me, and while growing up, he found no fault in my life. We never spoke on me, not being his son biologically. We didn't have to. He simply loved me like I was his own. Time was running out for him, and time was running out for me to thank him for stepping in when my biological father stepped out. That would have been an emotionally difficult conversation to have given the current situation. As a matter of choice, I let him know what he did for me as a man and not just as my father, but as a living example. At his bedside, he sensed that my tone and cadence were different. Like many men in his era, he was a very masculine man; he didn't express too many tender emotions. I've never seen my father cry, but that day when our eyes locked. I saw tears well up and hang on the edge of his eyelids as I spoke. He and I both knew what this moment meant for us. My daddy was the type of man that didn't worry about the outcome. He'd just move and get it done until the outcome came. He was the perfect example of the essential man. He never complained, never gave excuses, and he never quit. As I rambled on unpacking my emotions, our tears were like anxious racehorses ready to burst from their starting gates. But before one could fall, giving evidence to our emotions, I dabbed his tears away with the corner of my sleeve and laid my head on his chest, soaking my own tears into his hospital gown. I was glad to have shared that moment with my father because months later, he died. He loved me when he didn't have to. Like many other children with a step-up dad, they love without hesitation and are greater to someone else other than themselves. This man married my mother, raised me, gave me his last name, gave me security, gave me unconditional love and guidance. He never acted inappropriately around me, abused me, or made me to feel less than. Mr. James Garrett wasn't perfect, but he was perfect for me. He never made me feel like I was someone else's child or even mentioned it out of anger or otherwise. When my biological father dropped the ball, he stepped in, picked it up, tucked it away, and scored a touchdown. Through his actions, he taught me how to be my own man and what society would expect from me as a man. If his teachings were wrong, then I'd rather be wrong with him than right with my absent father. I've had a biological void growing up, but I didn't miss my biological father; how could I? I never knew him. I couldn't miss what I never had. He was a mystery man to me.

As an adult, I became a youth counselor and working with kids with similarities that aligned with traits of fatherless homes. I wanted to help out as much as possible, so I began to study, research, and speak to people to gain all the knowledge I could about the subject. In the process, I learned a lot about myself. Although I had a father that raised me, unfortunately, at times, he was absent himself. I realized that I suffered emotional abandonment from my step-up dad and physical abandonment from my biological father. I needed to find my purpose. Why am I here? Who am I? Who am I supposed to be? Questions like that floated in and out the majority of my childhood. While I searched for my own purpose, I attempted to give counsel to others searching for theirs. High school graduation was my first taste of true independence. I was free to do whatever I wanted to do. Continue education? Travel? Job core? Or Nothing at all? I chose to enlist in the U.S. Army while I figured it all out.

I saw the army as my stepping stone to my purpose. I saw men willingly giving their lives for other men. I wanted that. I wanted to be there for someone, and I wanted to know that someone was there for me. A band of brothers, a brotherhood between men that has given an oath never to abandon each other in the trenches. Much like a gang in inner-city neighborhoods. This was also one of my choices during my childhood, but it lacked the lure of integrity that I was looking for. However, I totally understand how young men join gangs to find their purpose through those bonds and brotherhoods. Young men need proving to be shown approved. The army turned out to be my proving ground. Hell, I even did my Advanced Individual Training at Aberdeen Proving Grounds, Maryland. It gave me structure, discipline, and a sense of responsibility to others. It was a source of resilience and strength, and I learned a lot about myself from my commanding officers. The service played father to many young people, transforming boys into men that were searching for their solid footing in life.

As children, we never know what our parents are protecting us from, but as adults, we now see. Single mothers have to find their Step-Up mate because its vitality important to the future of their children. About 16% of children worldwide live in a single-parent household. 12.9 million families in the U.S. were headed by a single parent, 80% of which were led by a female. Why wasn't my mother enough? Why did I feel the need to know my biological father? Why did I need a stranger to affirm me? Having my Step-Up father in my life, I had no reason to search for those answers, but as I aged, I found that my mother was enough, and I didn't necessarily need to know my biological father to succeed in life.

Many children mirror those same sentiments, but many more aren't so lucky. The consequence of a child having a father in the home versus a fatherless home I surmise is staggeringly dissimilar. In fact children with involved fathers are significantly more likely to excel in school, have higher self-esteem, and avoid high-risk and criminal behaviors compared to children who have uninvolved fathers. The probability of success for a child in a two-parent household is much greater than those raised by a single mother. It's simply beneficial to a child in his or her adult life to have a loving father in the home while growing up. I'm not concluding that a child raised by a single mother cannot succeed in their adult life. I'm simply applying the odds and the statistics to an overwhelming problem that can be traced back to a fatherless home. We, as adults, all benefited from what our parents allotted us. Most wouldn't trade that experience in for all the money in the world, while others would love to wipe the slate clean and start anew. Just imagine the children, now adults that had no fathers at all, that space had to be replaced by some type of father figure. Whether it was a gang, an uncle, a teacher, a coach, a mentor, or a friend. The influence from that appointed father figure is only a Band-Aid on an old fatherless wound. A wound that found a way to heal itself with a layer of skin. For the fatherless, that layer of skin can be depression, abandonment issues, emotional and behavioral problems, self-mutilation, suicide, drugs, or social ineptness. Hopefully, that Band-Aid or father figure was positive in nature and came early enough to help alleviate the problems that accompany fatherlessness at its conception. Most times, in a community with no fathers or positive father figures to emulate, the results can be detrimental for their future.

Good step-fathers, biological fathers, or foster parents are much better to have than not to have any father at all. The choices we make as adults directly decide what we experienced as children—whether it was happy, sad, or distant and abusive. The main focus is to connect the dots and find the root of our personalities and why we do the things we do. Some people need counseling to understand their lives, while others choose to figure it out along the way. People can overcome not having a father in their lives, but can't get over the feeling it leaves behind. Instead, they use his absence as fuel to be the best version of themselves, and that works. In chapters ahead, I give tools to thwart that dangerous dance of self-pity and guilt one can feel from time to time. Stop blaming yourself; stop blaming him or her. This is a condition that you can control. As you have read, many variables constitute the whys and the how comes of an absent father. That's not your fault; you can't control what others do. You can only control yourself and what you chose to believe about yourself.

For fathers that weren't around to raise their children, shame on you. If you're in jail for crimes you committed, that was your choice. For fathers who put their job before their children, again, it's a matter of choice. Find time to talk, visit, attend, and listen to the child you brought into this world. It's vitally important that you do this so that the child has a fighting chance and freedom of years of questions they cannot answer, for the fathers that felt that they couldn't get along with the mother of their children. I understand how your happiness is important, and being with the mother of your child isn't your idea of happiness. That doesn't mean you have the right to leave the child behind. You have a responsibility to that child, and it doesn't stop because you don't want the relationship with the baby's mother. At the end of the day, the choice was yours to make. Be a step-up dad and not just a man in your woman's' life. The children involved are watching and for them to become attached and then abandoned again is irresponsible on the part of the adults. Children will begin to lose trust in men as they grow up, and we will continue losing generations one broken heart at a time. Men need to get back to the men they were designed to be. Providing, loving, strong, protective, and most importantly, present. Not nomadic and roaming around like a rolling stone. Make a home and invite one woman in and create a family, stand by that family till the end. In turn that will send a wave of healing to the next generation and the generations to follow. Sampling different women like hors d'oeuvres, and leaving pieces of dipping sauce in each is not responsible; it's selfish. For those who believe that they have the income to support many kids, they're wrong. Money can't replace time spent with children. It's not about how many kids you can afford. It's about can you afford the time to spend with each kid. Don't be permanently temporary. Don't be that father that has kids stretched from town to town where they drop in to visit all the time temporarily. Men should understand the heavy responsibility in dating a single mother, and single mothers should be better stewards of whom they date. For the parents that lose a partner, there's nothing to be said. The death of a parent is hard to deal with within itself. Children will have an easier time accepting a father's death than that of a father that chose not to come around. That leaves an emotional stain that they cannot blot out with a conclusive end to their story. They usually find substitute fillers like artificial sweeteners instead of real sugar or tofu instead of meat to fill an absent father's spot. Hopefully, the one they choose to trust isn't an abuser. That's why being present to protect a child is only one of a father's jobs. The emptiness of not having a father present can last a lifetime. The sooner you realize it and take hold of the reality of his absence, the sooner you can heal and move forward emotionally. Some will say they're not affected by an absent father, but that's not true. Deep down inside, they feel it. Rather they know it or not, periodically that abandoning pain will show itself and will be quickly rejected. Over time they've learned how to band-aid that feeling, but it's hard to put a band-aid over a gashing wound. This book isn't a band-aid, but more or less like stitches to your wounds. Stop the bleeding, and let's sew this pain up.

How Fatherlessness Effects the Black & Brown Communities

What poses the biggest threat to the black community? The absence of black fathers! If Black America had an enemy, who or what would it be? Here's a better question; how would that enemy destroy the black community? Could it destroy them by giving them incurable diseases, much like what was done to the Indians with smallpox? Pack them into one area, then flood that living space with drugs and guns allowing them to destroy themselves? Create laws that unlawfully target them so that if those laws were broken, it'd put them away for an insane amount of years, stopping them from reproduction and or preventing them from properly raising their children? How about kill them, "legally" with over-policing and racial profiling? How about just giving them low to no education so they cannot make a proper living to support their families? Okay, okay, all that sounds like a horrible plot to a genocidal movie. The fact of the matter is, to the African-American family, it's called history. There have been some horrible, horrific things in American history against the black man, but the lasting one separates the black man from his family. This diabolical plot was detailed many years ago in the Willie Lynch Letter of 1712, titled The Making of A Slave! In part, it states:

"What do we need? First of all, we need a black nigger man, a pregnant nigger woman, and her baby nigger boy. Second, we will use the same basic principle that we use in breaking a horse, combined with some more sustaining factors. What we do with horses is that we break them from one form of life to another that is, we reduce them from their natural state in nature. Whereas nature provides them with the natural capacity to take care of their offspring, we break that natural string of independence from them and thereby create a dependency status, so that we may be able to get from them useful production for our business and pleasure. The Black slaves, after receiving this indoctrination shall carry on and will become self-refueling and self-generating for hundreds of years, maybe thousands..."

And for hundreds of years, it did last. Single parenting in the black community didn't just appear. It was manufactured, planted, passed down psychologically. For many black Americans, the emotional and psychological imprints of that deplorable mental breaking of our ancestry have lasted longer than the physical abuses that were abjectly used upon them in those moments. In the entire recorded history of the planet, there's never been a greater voluntary abandonment of men from their children than there is in black America. In Baby Moma Monique's case, raising her boys alone isn't as foreign to the black communities as one would think. Many men and women will tell you that their mothers or grandmothers raised them. Throughout history, black mothers have been raising children on their own, not to mention raising children that's not their own for decades. Whether it was as slaves, housemaids, surrogates, nannies, or nursemaids, it's been a lifetime of nurturing from the black mother. So where are the black fathers? Stereotypes will suggest that they don't love their children as much as the other races. This is absolutely not true. Black men care and love their children as much as any other race of human beings on the planet, sometimes to the death of them. History will show that African wars were fought and won for the well-being of the family. What happened between now and then was systematic and all-out cruel without going as far back as slavery. The most ingenious breakdown of family was implemented into the black community. I'll attempt to break it down for you, and maybe you'll get some sense of where these stereotypes derived from. Statics show that fatherlessness is a problem not just in the black and brown communities, but across America. 15% Asian, 24% White, 41% Hispanic, or Latino live in fatherless homes, today the American Indian sits at 53%, but it's the black children who are leading the race at an alarming rate of 65%.

The uncaused first cause of the beginning of the universe didn't know there would be a separation in cultures among blacks and whites. Systemic racism has a lot to do with generational set-backs.

It isn't exclusively economical. When you tie together systemic oppression, economic depression with the lack of public support, progression in those communities will suffer. The truth is poverty will continue to increase in poor communities all over the country. The have-nots will always want what the haves got, but race has played a major part in the digression of equality. The American dream wasn't meant for the black and brown communities. They were always told to 'Pull yourself up by your bootstraps.' which meant to improve your situation on your own merits without any aid. This is the antithesis to the statement because the oppressors kidnapped Africans from their homeland, brought them to America, forced them into free labor to build wealth for over 400 years, then set them free with no land, no money, or any percentage in any developments that they contributed to. Then they tell the next generation of African Americans to stop complaining and make way for themselves. The economic, educational, and social starting line for the black community was set 400 years back when the progressive starting whistle was blown. The black race is a resilient one, but the moment our complaining stopped, and construction began, the rules would shift, fairness and equality was thrown out the door.

Black Wall Street comes to mind when I think about a community on the rise of social progression and having a steady increase of wealth, but was all destroyed by racial violence. It was when whites burned down a whole town of an affluent black community because it was seen as a threat to white-dominated capitalism. Please read the stories on race massacres that devastated black communities across America, such in places like Colfax Louisiana (1873), Wilmington North Carolina (1898), Atlanta Georgia (1906), Elaine Arkansas (1919), and Rosewood, Florida (1923). That setback in Tulsa, Oklahoma, in 1921 erased generations of progression for the African American family. Those atrocities don't account for the black fathers separated from their families because they were killed or sold off to other plantations. So, when did the black fathers stop raising black sons and daughters? What happened between then and now?

In the '60s and '70s, it was the deindustrialization of our communities, unemployment, and other socioeconomic problems that led to the breakdown of families in the community. Even if a family wanted to move out of the ghetto, it was very difficult. Lenders wouldn't lend, and sellers weren't selling, redlining the blacks to restrict them from moving into predominantly white neighborhoods. This red-lining method limited blacks to attain loans, thus keeping them segregated. The few who tried were met with intense hostility and violence. Throughout hub cities like Detroit, Baltimore, and Chicago, were abandoned factories, vacant houses, closed storefronts where the black community depended on for economic survival. Black people didn't need any college degrees to secure those jobs; they just had to work hard and climb up the corporate ladder. But when those factories in those communities shut down, the men were left jobless, homeless, and powerless. Then came along welfare policies to help pick up the slack, but in actuality, it played a major role in a rise in fatherless homes. The president at the time, Ledon B. Johnson, aka LBJ, was even quoted when referencing the black Americans "I will give them enough to survive, but not enough to make a difference..." And the difference was, with a then liberal government and the rise of feminism, made it to where the black woman didn't need the black man in the home. Those who tried keeping the man in the home and still attempting to collect welfare checks would live in constant fear of a social worker catching him there and losing the entire financial assistance. Instead of welfare policy, it would have been better for the black community to receive tax incentives for parents with kids that share the same address. These steps would have ensured that social policies did not discourage marriage, but rather encourage it.

The '80s tried to make a comeback with some advantages in education, but the single black woman was still leading the household. The children from those homes were at greater risk of joining gangs, dropping out of school, teen pregnancy, going to jail, and not to mention the mental and emotional abuses it left. Then in the '90s came the most aggressive generational problem, the influx of crack cocaine. People would steal, kill, and destroy themselves for this drug. Those who used it were no good to the community, and those who sold it were locked up for an infinite number of years, leaving a trail of fatherless homes. It's no secret that black families suffered the most with the introduction of crack. While former First Lady Nancy Regan said, "Just say no to drugs." her presidential husband, Ronald Regan, and the CIA allowed drugs to flood the inner-city. It made some teenagers rich at the peril of destroying the community around them, and in the end, they were murdered in the process or went to jail. Depressed and struggling, commoners began to use the drug and lost the little they did have and the hope they ever had to a better life. Many crack users gave birth to crack babies, leaving the babies with an inherited potpourri of physical and mental problems. The families that didn't use and were on the path of betterment were surrounded by walking zombies, strung out neighbors, friends, extended family members, or classmates. Drug pushers became drug users, nice homes became crack houses, and the working class began to crumble. Either side of the drug argument you chose, you lose. Users were unproductive and slowly dying, and sellers were gunned down or sent to jail in the process.

To this day, there are families still recouping from the residue of causalities that crack left behind. One of which is the children left fending for themselves. Two generations of progression in the black community were set back 30 years. It left children in those areas living with a grandmother, or an aunt, managing paycheck to paycheck, and when she dies, that child will inherit her assets, which were only sentimental in value. They would live the same way, check to check, because they were taught no different. It perpetuates itself; learned behavior begets learned behavior. To break that poverty cycle, some kids would take the risk of making fast money, so when those children came into a little extra money, they would buy drugs to resell and make more money in hopes of eventually breaking that poverty cycle. For most, it's never a way out. It's a way in.

In jail, in the grave, in debt, or stuck in a revolving door of unknowing. There weren't enough positive male influences around to guide these young black children to an alternative way out. For most, their golden ticket out of the ghetto was a sports or entertainment contract. As we well know, every child couldn't jump high or sing and dance, so it left a gap of unknowingness for those who didn't make it to college or didn't make it in entertainment. So, it's not hard to imagine how in today's society, there are adults walking around that grew up without a father in the home. Some would say, "So what there's no father in the home, those hoodlums chose to sell drugs or participate in crimes. We as a society need to hold them accountable."

In some cases, that could be true, and we as a society do hold them accountable, but what we fail to realize is that not having a father's guidance and a solid family structure has hindered the development of our young black and brown youth. It's no secret that teen pregnancy, drugs, and the number of dropouts is higher in the black and brown communities. That results in poor to no education, which equals to a limited earning potential and an overall low quality of life. Essentially, these particular fathers began with good intentions that eventually faded. They more than likely grew up in a fatherless home themselves. The weak attachments to their community, limited education and skills, low earnings, and the impact of racism didn't make things any easier.

In today's brown communities, the threat of deportation of fathers, keeping them from their children, or detaining them for months and sometimes years at a time. This is a separation tactic that the government has used for years. For a family to make a better life for themselves, they migrate to places where they'll have a better chance of survival. Then in order to stay, they must work and make a living. If children are produced within that time, the children are citizens of that country, so when the parents are deported, the children are left to fend for themselves. Some are required to go to detention camps, but under the harsh living conditions and lack of proper aid, some migrant children died. These and similar events can psychologically affect a person and a person's entire life. I'm no politician, but things concerning these matters must be addressed and changed before we have a whole society of disgruntled, depressed, stressed out children that will soon be disgruntled, depressed, and stressed out adults.

Growing up with a father in the home adds protection to a child from possible psychological, emotional, and physical abuse. Not to say that him being in the home will eliminate those abuses, but it will give the child a physical example of how to deal with them if they were to arise. Children in the lower black communities already have enough problems with gangs, drugs, economic stresses, and subpar education. Not having a father in the home only worsens their situation. Right outside their door on their doorsteps are issues too big for them to navigate without a proper male compass. A mother can tell her boy what to do and how to act, but that little boy needs to see for himself how a man acts and reacts to pressures. Without those examples he will search out and find his own example of what he thinks a man is and how one should act. It's not a far stretch to say that in those impoverished neighborhoods that the gang members, the drug pushers, and hustlers are part of those examples. To a young mind seeing negative examples of men outside their doorsteps via social media sets a new bar of success for them in their neighborhood. They see their friends acting foolishly, and they want to fit right in and do it as well. They see that other men are cosigning their behavior so it couldn't be all bad. They're sadly mistaken, and without the proper tools, a young man can foolishly be impressed by and have an affinity to those type of men. Within a small window of time, those affections for that ill-type lifestyle can be detrimental to their lives. There are many graves and plenty of jails full of young boys that sought out father figures and found a cellmate or a hospital bed instead. By the time that ghetto success nostalgia wears off, it's too late to recapture the innocence that was lost. It's a revolving door of boys looking for men to show them how to be men. These boys shouldn't have to look past their very own fathers for guidance, self-worth, structure, and love.

Young girls are not exempt from needing a father and his love and guidance. Instead, they seek that missing father in romantic relationships, whether it's toxic or meritorious. They'll attempt to fill that hole in their heart with relationships. Young girls and some women will stay in bad relationships and accept bad behavior from men because it's the only love they've experienced from a man. They never had a father around to show them how to love a man and, more importantly, how a man should love them. Their definition of love is defined by immature boys and not men, thereupon creating an endless search for a father's love in relationships that many women fail to find.

As a consequence of not having a father in the home, it can lead to early sexual activity and increase the probability of adolescent pregnancy. This can be very problematic for a single parent already struggling to raise their child. Imagine raising your kids under stressful economic conditions with looming gang affiliation for your son and early pregnancy for your daughter. These are real tangential scenarios sprinkling the black communities, and the prime solution lies with the missing father.

Now, I don't want to paint the entire black community and its youth with a broad brush because everyone isn't involved in gangs, doing drugs, or pregnant. Undesirable mentionable happens in every community, but the fact of the matter is, the black community is a thriving community where people are doing amazing things. Children go to school, parents raise their children together, and black men are perfect examples of what men should be. The gangs that live among them are a direct result of failed parenting and, in most cases, birthed from single-parent homes. The African-American citizens that live among gang members, sexual predators, drug sellers, and users themselves need protection from these deviants. The media gather same topic storylines and perpetuate fear in those communities. So, it's easy for an outsider to assume that most black youths are gang members, thugs, drug dealers, or menaces to their community. Of course, when people that are not familiar or have minimal encounters with young black youth, they'll have a certain fear of them and subsequently unconsciously treat them differently. At times, the media weaponized their storylines to get the result of whatever agenda they set forth. Whether negative or positive, the light it shines on the black and brown communities are iniquitous and biased. Their subliminal programming of negative stereotypes and indoctrination is obvious. Writers, filmmakers, and brand creators grab ideas from those lopsided agendas and use them to tell stories of what they perceive the black families are like.

In entertainment past and present, the average black family has been portrayed as a broken, dysfunctional, and flawed configuration. Early on in television, it was a long-running fact that the black father was not to be in the home with his family for a show to make a successful run until The Cosby Show. The Cosby Show is about an auspicious black working mother and father raising their kids together in a loving household. They had normal problems like the rest of America, none of which were without wisdom, sound advice, and love from their parents. The show was an automatic hit. It displayed black families in a different light. It put America on notice and announced that all black people weren't living in the ghetto and weren't all uneducated or undereducated. It tackled familiar topics that were not just attached to black families, but to all families. It gave an insight into what the joy of raising a family gives. People loved it; TV Guide ranked it the biggest hit television show of the eighties. It was the first of its kind in the way of giving America a peek on the inside of a functional American black family. It wasn't always like that. Shows that came before it always had some negative connotation attached to it, and America took that as a fact when looking into the black family. Some writers, producers, and heads of networks were wedded to this false narrative of the black family, and their agendas were clear, it showed in the content they released.

Eric Monte, one of the creators of a hit show in the seventies called Good Times, speaks to it. It was a show based around a poor black couple raising their three kids in the ghetto of Chicago. Eric gives an account of the agendas set forth by studio heads: During the time of trying to get the show on the air for three years, time and time again, the running notes from production meetings were, "You have to get rid of the father, a strong black man doesn't work in a sitcom." They wanted it to be a matriarchic family, which is a family ran by the woman. America wouldn't buy it otherwise. Needless to say, after the show ran for six years. For those that remember the show, the episode that shocked the viewers most was the death of the father, James Evans, played by John Amos. "Damn, damn, damn." was all that was painfully uttered from his wife, Florida Evans, played by Esther Role when she received the tragic news of his passing on this epic episode. That episode left the black community speechless. The show continued for three more seasons without a father and a single mother raising two boys and a girl, our society's definition of the norm. The black viewers watching these images and were following these storylines had little to no hope in the surety of black men leading a household.

On-screen, the black father was always portrayed to be uneducated, absent, or some sort of criminal. This gave a misconception of the black family to other cultures. Is there some truth to it? Some. Black families were in destitute situations that had to make things work because the father wasn't there, but to only see that representation of black people on screen all the time was a hard pill to swallow. I remember seeing an interview by Ed Gordon on the iconic rapper, Tupac Shakur. Tupac pretty much summed it up as single mothers raised most of the kids in neighborhoods he visited. Tupac had to learn lessons the hard way, and if he had a father around, people would see and hear it in his behavior and his responses to tough times. He recants, *"There are some lessons that I missed along the way, and you can see the lessons that I missed when you talk to me, you can see where I didn't have a father when you talk to me, you can see I spent a lot of my time in the streets when you talk to me because the words I say don't come from a mother's mouth or a father's mouth. It's words that come from a pimp's mouth or a prostitute or a hustler or a drug dealer. To me, these were my role models."* Ed asks, "How did that affect you?" Tupac replies, *"...Had I had a father. I would have helped my mother more. She wouldn't have gone the road she went* (drugs, gangs, joining the Black Panther Party). *I could have been a better son. She wouldn't had went that road. It was the absence of my father. I'm dealing with daddy not being there, and my mother is dealing with her man not being there. It's so many problems in our community that affects everything..."* His father, not being in his life, clearly affected this young man's future, which was how he saw things. At times, he was angry, lost, broken, scared, depressed, and it reflected in his musical and theatrical genius. That missing father piece had an emotional and intellectual impact not only in Tupac's life but a whole generation of black children with missing fathers. It's a hole that can't be filled with just words. Young men need to see examples of it. They seek it out like the adolescent male lion roaming the Savannah looking for his pride, his place, his self.

A young black man's ego is so fragile. It's not because they are emotionally fragile in general, but to them, to appear weak only invites abuse from bullies, predators, molesters, or anyone that want to do them harm. Telling young men that they have to be tough is just another myth that surrounds men in general. They don't have to be tough. They have to be discerning of their strength. Knowing why and when times call for toughness can build good character and be life-changing in certain situations. It's one thing to be strong and have strength in moments where it's needed, but to walk around with a chip on your shoulder can only invite trouble. Young black men living in rough communities feel it to be mandatory for them to walk around with that chip, or else they'll become prey to predators. But even from the toughest to the weakest black man, some things leapfrog their egos, and that's trying to emasculate them. Attempting to take away their manhood will not be tolerated on any level, and anything that hints at it will be met with resistance. That's a form of power that black and brown children aren't willing to give up. It's one thing to tell them to turn another cheek, but a whole other thing to make them feel less than. In the black community, certain violations will set them off in this. These violations would warrant a fight, the N-word (which represents that they're less than the user of the word), and the other is speaking ill of someone's mother. Even when joking, that can halt all the jokes, because for most young black men and women, their mothers were the most precious asset they had. The last violation is one that silently hurts young black men, and the response would be immediate, but the pain would be time-released and that's speaking truth about them not knowing their real fathers. That phrase would simmer anger and frustration, there was nothing they could do, because the truth hurts. The feeling of powerlessness is something no one can ignore. It's simply nothing you can do about it. They don't want to ever again have the sense of being powerless, so they become powerful to ensure it. Joining up with or surrounding themselves with others that mirror that same energy. Some children with absent fathers go to the military to find that missing piece, some to college, some enter sports, and unfortunately, some even go to jail seeking some sort of guidance and acceptance. At times children feel the need for acceptance, which drives them to act out at school or in public for attention. Unaware of the consequences that their actions will have in those moments. When we tear away the layers of social constructs and behavioral paroxysm, we find, at its core, the creation of this false wall of toughness to protect their emotions. When in actuality, all they want is immediate love and acceptance from someone that looks like them, a father.

When we speak on the black community, it usually concerns our youth and or violence. People are meant to believe that it's solely black on black crime that's killing our youth, but that's not true. There is indeed a problem with kids killing kids, but there’s no black on black crime, that’s an antonym, it's poor on poor crime in our neighborhoods. In white neighborhoods, the majority of crimes against them will be from a person that looks like them. This is true in all communities of the same race. So why do black people get this special title, black on black crime? Black people associated with violence and self-hatred is not a known trope like our country has portrayed it to be. Community violence is in every community, but structured violence only lies in the black and brown communities. Structured as in police brutality, unsolved murders, and uninvestigated abuses. The overall message to young black youth from a quiet America is that "If you don't make us comfortable, we will kill you." That's hard to tell your children what's outside the doors of their already broken home. The skin that black kids are born in is an immutable trait that cannot and should not be changed. We have to tell our children that their skin can omit a threat response in another human being that causes them to feel justified in taking their lives. (i.e., George Floyd in 2020, he was casually suffocated by a police officer with a knee on his throat as the world witnessed this modern-day lynching or an Ahmaud Arbery, a young man out for a jog in Georgia gets shot down in the street by white citizens.) It's sad, but it's the world we live in right now. Black single mothers not only have to raise their children alone with little to no support, but they should also have a fearful awareness of their children being hurt when they leave their homes. That's hard for any parent to live with. Mothers of black kids are the same as the mothers of white kids because all they want is their children to be safe. The difference between the two is the conversation each has to have with their children before leaving the comfort of their home. Black mothers have to have a different dialogue with their kids regarding being out in society. They're told that the public will see the color of their skin before they know the content of their character. So they're told not to wear hooded sweat shirts or certain colors, and not to keep their hands in their pockets when approached by law enforcement, and not to commune with two or more other black teens, and not to protest even if it's right, and not to play their music too loud or play with toy guns in the park or department stores. (These are all real-life examples of ways black kids were unlawfully killed in recent years) Black mothers want to keep their children safe, but at the same time, they don't want to break their spirit and restrict their freedom. It can rob children of the innocence of being a kid solely because America is devaluing them. Mothers have to tell their kids that their clothes silently communicate who they are and may indicate aggression to those that don't know them. In black communities, their clothes can get them killed and outside their communities, and just being black can get them killed.

Every teen out of the black community is not a thug, a super predator, or in a gang, but most gang members come from father-absent homes. One could argue that a gang member can also come out of a neglectful two-parent household just as well. I'm not diametrically opposed to that conclusion, but I believe the odds weigh heavily on the fact that there's a direct correlation between gangs and father-absent homes. If the parents aren't giving the love to the child as he/she needs it, that child will seek it elsewhere. Living in a community flooded with other neglected kids with idle time, the chances are he/she will eventually join together, like a brotherhood. They didn't necessarily join or be a part of this brotherhood to be a menace, but to simply find an emotionally safe place. Their peers are someone they can relate to, who cares and understands what they're going through. Usually, their home lives are grossly similar, so their connections are fluid. If you remember,

I listed the consequences of a fatherless home and two in particular deals specifically with black and brown children more than the rest. That is the number of children dropping out of school and their criminal involvement. A person doesn't have to be fatherless to engage in criminal activities or to give up on their education, but the likelihood of both increases without a father in the home. There are plenty of reasons why kids drop out of school, but being racially profiled while walking the hallways shouldn't be one of them. Yes, there are some kids that get into trouble at school simply for fitting the profile or, in lament terms, for being black.

Schools use a structure of codes and punishments that criminalizes kids as earliest as pre-school. This early introduction of harsh authority programs children and increases their chances of ending up in the criminal justice system. Or the Just-Us System, because to the African-American and Latino communities, it's just us that are disproportionately being incarcerated and ultimately killed. I read a book written by Douglas A. Blackmon called "Slavery by Another Name." It's a story set in the 1800s; the writer describes how the police would harass and falsely accuse blacks of petty crimes to lock them up. Then charge them a fine they most certainly could not pay. Therefore, they would be sentenced into forced labor. Sounds familiar?

In some schools, children are psychologically groomed for forced labor. Bars on the windows, guards patrolling the campuses, everything ran off the bell system. The unfair policing, suspensions and punishment of black students are only harming them and not helping. Sometimes the offense could be as minimal as being late to class or doodling on a desk. In urban schools, misbehaved kids could get handcuffed and searched regularly. Some are even abused and drug out by the hair. It's the same thing that happens to them or people that look like them on the streets. Even if their offense doesn't end up in an arrest, the punishment is still harsher than that of their white peers. The adultification of black and brown children in the judicial system has been grossly biased in comparison to their white counterparts. Sometimes misbehavior can be interpreted as a cry for help across the nationality board, but in the black and brown communities, their children's cry for help is slapped with stiff sentencing and probation. While other ethnicities cry for help are remedied with counseling and therapy. It's not a set up for freedom, but a setback into failure. Millennial dismissiveness and the lack of respect for rules, schools tend to prosecute students for pre-delinquent behavior. Pre-delinquent behavior? So even before there's delinquent behavior, a student can be sent to detention or put on some type of probation? This is another way to program black and brown children into fear-based thinking instead of encouraging ambition. How can they excel in school if they're always getting kicked out of them? Expelling kids, keeping them out of school, and sending them back to their neighborhoods with idle hands is in actuality a cover-up to funneling them into prisons. It's called the School to Prison Pipeline. When Bill Clinton was president, there was an influx of mass incarceration. The last time that I checked, it was 2,236,800 adults in the U.S. Justice System, not to mention 4,540,000 of them under supervision or probation. Prisons are a business, and like any other business, they're in it for the money, and the money comes with bodies in cells and free labor. Corporations own prisons, and their stocks are publicly traded upon. The housing cost of an inmate is estimated at $68,000 a year. Almost equaling the cost of tuition at a prestigious college. Institutions pay inmates .08 cents/hr. for a job that they would pay a qualified citizen up to $20-30 an hour, saving a ton of money and making even more on the labor. During President Obama's term, there was a de-funding of private prisons. That slowed down the constructions of some prisons in certain states, but incarceration is growing at such a rapid pace that it's metastasizing in the black community. Our institutions are as strong as the people who comprise them. Many of our institutions have people in them with some backward values and outdated thinking. That way of thinking isn't bringing this country together, instead it's dividing us further apart. Slavery is no longer legal, but cheap labor is far game. Undocumented citizens will do jobs for close to no money, and prisoners are forced to do it for even a lower pay. The people who invest in and vote for these institutions tend to benefit the most. The lawmakers and lobbyists are in cahoots with each other and will not do anything that will compromise their bottom line. So regardless of innocence or guilt, and regardless of due process or time matching the crimes committed. The order has been set forth to fill up their prisons, and just like the 1800s, they continue to get free labor. It's clear as day the disparity of justice that's being administered to young black and brown men, and it strongly leans towards systematic incarceration through the School-to-Prison pipeline.

My mother, a retired educator, wrote in our family's 2015 Beasley Family Reunion bulletin: "But today, the business that topped all agendas was providing the needs of Marc, Pat, Craig, Pamela, and Kianna. What took first place was keeping their self-esteem in place. Some schools and teachers make children feel less than their abilities. But the role of the home is to restore their children and allow their talents to be developed. Children, too, need wings." Thank God for a mother that gave us wings of confidence and surety that if we fell, we would be alright. When kids are constantly suspended from school, they eventually stop going, and research suggests that they're three times more likely to end up in a juvenile justice system within a year. It's all part of an endless cycle because once kids touch juvie, 67% of them end up back in jail before they're 25. Most of the time, they'll let young people that are silently screaming for help destroy themselves.

Put them in jail for a small stint, then parole them out only to violate that parole and be put back in for an even longer sentence.

Imagine you're on a farm and raising chickens, then you set those chickens free into the neighboring fields. Those chickens would have nowhere to go, no skills to survive, or any rooster or hens (parents) to guide them. Therefore, it's not inconceivable to believe that the chickens will meander around those captive cages and even climb back into the environment from which it was familiar with. Being a young man, unguided, uneducated, and unknowing of how detrimental his actions can do to his future is unfair to his existence. For children that are raised in urban areas, all they know is bars on their homes, bars at their local stores, bars at their schools, to bars in jail. They're slowly being programmed to normalize being caged and monitored. Once you treat children like animals while incarcerated, you can't be surprised that they act like animals when they get out in order to survive. Without rehabilitation or reform for them inside those walls, they'll simply get out to commit another crime and the powers that be will gladly stick them back into forced labor of the newly upgraded plantation, jail.

I sat in on the sentencing of a young man; he couldn't have been any more than 20 years old. He stood alone, without a lawyer, before a female judge. A bulky bailiff shadowed him nearby. The court reporter typed away, emotionless. Family members in the audience sobbed. I couldn't tell if they were there to support the young man or the family members of the victim. To me, it didn't matter whose tears they were because both families will be affected by the irrational decision this young man-made. I didn't know his crimes, but it had to be heinous in nature because the death penalty was on the table. As I sat there, I watched the court operate business as usual, papers being passed about, public defenders and lawyers whispering to each other, and even a few scoffs of laughter between them. All the while, this young man's life was in the balance. I wondered about his story and how he was raised, and what led him to be in this place. By his appearance, he looked harmless, innocent, and scared, but we all know that looks can be deceiving. I felt sorry for him because he was alone, lost, and naive about what was happening to him. He stood motionless as the judge spoke. He replied politely to her questions with, "Yes, ma'am and no ma'am." Then the judge handed down the sentence accompanied by some stern words. This is where I realized the revolving door of fatherlessness is the real-life sentence. She read off the crimes, and I learned that it was the murder of a store clerk. She continued saying, "But there was no remorse, just saying you're sorry doesn't make it so. You're not sorry for what you did, yet. Maybe someday you will be. You weren't sorry that day you committed the crime. You weren't sorry when you took the stand, and you're not sorry now. Your son will grow up without a father, just as you did. But worse than you, he will grow up without a father, because he will know the crimes you did was selfish and didn't have him in your future. Hopefully, with the love he has from other family members, he'll grow up a happy, healthy, productive, and loving person, but that won't be because of you. And based on the decision of the jury on all counts, I sentence you to life in prison without the possibility of parole." This blew my mind on how much life that young man will never live and how potentially damaging it will be for his son.

A father gives a child a sense of respect for authority. In the urban community, his discipline is love. In his absence, so goes the respect for authority. How do we get that back? One way is to get fathers to stay in the homes and raise their kids, but in the case of absent fathers, it's going to take a village. That doesn't only apply to family or extended family members. It applies to teachers, counselors, preachers, mentors, entertainers, sports figures, servicemen, and women as well. Coming down with an iron fist isn't always the answer to discipline. I understand that law enforcement has a very difficult job patrolling urban areas. Still, it has been shown consistently that over-policing the community has created distrust within the community it's designed to protect. All they see them as is enforcers and no longer protcctors, which makes them no longer respect the police and take the law into their own hands. It perpetuates itself to a re-accruing cycle of predator and prey to the entire black and brown communities. The inner city does need policing, but it can do without police brutality. The solution. Have the officers connect more with the community that they're policing. Meaning, not only patrol the block but also talk to people, share a story or two, connect. Regain community trust, which will solve more crimes in the long run. This could possibly prevent a teenager from committing a crime because that officer met his mom, or maybe that officer themselves won't fear every young man with a hooded sweatshirt on because they recognize who's under the hoodie before they approach. Lots can come from truly interacting more with the community they serve. For those officers who want overtime, have them go into the schools and meet those kids that are in detention or go to the homes of the ones that were suspended and show them that they are important and not insignificant. I wrote this book as a preemptive strike against the war we have against the effects of fatherlessness in urban and sub-urban households across America. There are ways to extinguish this school to prison funneling, but again it will take all of us in this communal village of life.

Finding Him. The Hurts & The Healing of It All

The moment I decided I was going to find him. I did. My mother and biological fathers' story is theirs and theirs alone. I'm a product of their union, and whatever back-story they had with each other had nothing to do with me. I had no say, no opinion, no voice in the forming of me. I just needed to put a face to the voices in my head and hush the louder voices asking, "Why wouldn't he want to meet me?" At the very least, why wouldn't he want to even know about me? I was determined to prove to him that I turned out to be a great kid, someone who would be proud to call me their son. I felt as though I had to show him all the things he missed out on and prove that I wasn't a mistake, but a gift.

This moment reminded me of a movie I saw, "Creed."It was the 4th adaption of the Rocky franchise. The character Apollo Creed was in the 1st Rocky movic and was Rockys' nemesis in his heavyweight title debut. Rocky showed perseverance in a close hard fought match. Fast forward to the movie Creed, Apollo Creed had a son named Adonis. His father Apollo died in the ring in a bloody match with this Russian heavyweight, so Adonis was raised fatherless. He rotated from one foster home to the next. He had a very troubled childhood, getting involved in all types of criminal activities. He resented everything that made him feel attached. His hard exterior and tough demeanor showed that he didn't need anyone or anything. But it was clear to the viewers that he longed for a father and felt as though the world owed him something for taking his father away. Rocky, played by Sylvester Stallone, agreed to train Adonis and be in his corner for his title fight. Throughout the movie, we see that Adonis' defensive walls begin to soften, and he attaches himself to Rocky. He even refers to him as "Unc," short for uncle, giving him a closer bond than just a friend or acquaintance. As this film plays out, we see that it doesn't matter how a child becomes fatherless; the traits of their upbringing will transfer into their adulthood. So, in Creed, Adonis is in the fight of his life, he's being beaten up pretty bad and on the verge of losing the fight, but his determination keeps him in the contest.

Ex-champ, trainer, and now cornerman, Rocky wants to throw in the towel like he should have done with Adonis' dad Apollo Creed when he was in his corner. He blames himself for not stopping the fight back then. With one eye swollen shut, bruised ribs, bleeding, battered, and hanging on by a string. Adonis tells Rocky not to stop the fight because he wants to prove his worth. Rocky is bewildered at the statement and says, "Prove what?" Adonis replies, "That I wasn't a mistake." His old fatherless wounds were open and bleeding all over that statement. I connected with those words when I searched for my own father. As adults, we want to prove that we weren't mistakes, accidents, or dirty little inconveniences. We need to feel wanted and not discarded. Finding and connecting with our fathers could be the essential piece in our healing.

Coming from a large family in a bible belt community, I can only imagine the stress of the underlying chatter my mother had to endure. She had a brother living in Los Angeles, so she packed up my older brother and I, and we moved. I was only a toddler at the time, but she tells me that when she got to California, she met the perfect man, they fell in love, got married, and had three more children, which made us a complete family. Mr. James Garrett was the only father I ever knew, I was too young to realize that he was not my biological father, but at the time, it didn't matter because the love he gave us was consistent across the board. I never had any feelings of exclusion. I always felt included and a part of, but let me share the day I found out my father wasn't my father.

Growing up, like many other families, we would entertain guests with big books stuffed with photos, vacation bible school certificates, faded flowers, ticket stubs from concerts, etc. Those photo albums were that eras social media. It was how you could share experiences, memorable moments, and special events with friends and guests. When I wasn't outside playing with my friends, I would be perched up on the couch, flipping through those albums. Tons of pictures of my southern relatives, my siblings and I as babies, our outings, and my parent's wedding pictures. On many occasions, my mom and I would sit together, and she would tell me all the stories behind the pictures. It was always a fun family history lesson that she would share with us. Instead of having my mother read me a children's book before bed, I would pull out one of those photo albums, and we'd walk down memory lane. This particular day, I remember leaning up against my mother with her arm wrapped around me as she turned the pages. We stopped at her wedding pictures. I asked many questions about everybody in the pictures and who they were and what connection they had to us in the family. I had a rapid-fire round of questions, and each one was leading to the next. That was the moment my mother told me the story of my biological father.

As a child, I didn't immediately weigh feelings about it or really understood what it meant. Later in years, I would find myself daydreaming about him, what he was like, who he was, and how that affected me. These feelings would periodically haunt me my whole life. The feeling it would give me was similar to walking into a movie late. Action is happening, the plot is set, characters are talking, but I had no clue on what's going on. I had a bunch of questions like, who is that character, why is he doing that, and how did they get there? All while people around me are being frustrated and shushing me the whole time. Like, get over it, you turned out fine, be quiet about that, just watch the movie. So, for many years, I did. I didn't speak about my feelings with my younger siblings or to anybody. The only time it would come up was with my mother, whenever she would reference that I was just like him. That only peeked my curiosity as I grew older. It wasn't until I was 27 years old before I decided to reach out to him again. I wrote a couple of more letters that were unanswered. I called the only number I had on him that would never get picked up. It was disappointing, to say the least, but I would tell myself it didn't matter, and I didn't care if he doesn't write back or pick up the phone because "I gotta daddy."

When in actuality, it absolutely burned a hole in my heart that I was totally being ignored and trying my best to forget about. That burning in me wouldn't be quenched until I found him. Searching for a father is like playing Hide & Seek with your friends, but instead, you're playing a real-life game of searching for your father. After having my eyes closed and counting for 27 years, my heart was ready to scream out, "Ready or not, here I come!". I was searching for him for hours, days, months, years to no avail. During this time of searching, there were feelings of constant anticipation at every turn, "Is that him?" only to be let down once again. Being rejected hurts at all ages, and to avoid that feeling, years would go by before I even tried again. That desire to know my father was an inextinguishable flame that burned deep inside me for years. In that children's game I described, when the searcher gives up their search, they can opt-out and give up. They can yell out a pre-agreed phrase "Olly Olly oxen free" or in other words, "I can't find you, and it is safe for you to come out of hiding." There are millions of searching children and adults screaming at the top of their lungs, "Olly olly oxen free!" to their biological fathers to which their cries are grossly unanswered.

I remember cutting a picture of him out of my mother's college yearbook. I kept that small cutout in my wallet for many years. He looked just like me, head shaped like mine, and even had a quirky smile on his face similar to expressions I've displayed in some of my grade school portraits. I'd often stare at it, studying his face, imaging how his voice would sound, and what kind of mannerisms he would have. Was he tall or short, funny or brash? I needed to know. A part of me felt some sense of disloyalty to my present father. Breezes of guilt and hints of ungratefulness swept pass me when I was searching for a father that didn't want me when I had a father that did. Those unsettling feelings battled inside me periodically throughout my whole life, but I couldn't share those concerns with my siblings, so I kept my quest for my biological father covert. My only ally in this was my mother, but even around her, I would reserve those emotions.

Every year my family travels from California to Texas for our family reunion. It was then when I took advantage of meeting my biological father. I didn't tell anyone when or where I was going, so I couldn't ask for a ride or where things were. There weren't any ride-shares or GPS at the tip of my fingers at the time, so I had to map out a bus route with the only address I had in hand. The address I had was to his workplace, a local pharmacy chain, about an hour away. So, with his picture in my wallet and a photo album I put together of my childhood he missed in my lap, I sat on a city bus rehearsing much of what I wanted to say. A roller coaster of emotions whirled in and out of me for the entire trip. At one point, I almost got off the bus and called the whole thing off. Fortunately, all those years of that burning curiosity kept my butt planted in my seat until it was time to exit. When I arrived at my stop, and I saw the pharmacy across the street, I immediately felt butterflies in my stomach as if I was going on a first date. My hands got clammy, throat got dry, and my speech got choppy. "Ah...um...is this my stop?". The loud sound of air compression swung the door open, and my heart began to beat faster as I exited the city bus. I didn't go right into the pharmacy. I stood on the side of the building, taking it all in and reassuring myself that it's okay if he doesn't accept me. As I walked into the pharmacy, everything went into slow motion, and all my senses seemed heightened times a thousand. The senor ding at the entrance sounded to me like an enormous chime from a clock tower. I could smell cleaning products on the floor as if it were freshly mopped, and I could feel every single ridge of my photo album shifting in my sweaty palms. I'm not sure if anyone noticed my nervousness, but I felt like the whole state of Texas knew that I was there looking for my father. A female technician greeted me in a southern voice, "Good afternoon and welcome." I was a deer caught in headlights. I didn't reply with words, my throat was too dry, but I did manage to crack a crooked smile through my teeth. For a person outside looking in, I probably appeared to be someone about to rob the place. Standing on the side of the building, sweaty and nervous, head down, not speaking. I was a suspicious wreak. I didn't want to cause any disruption in his workplace or his life for that matter. I just wanted closure. I started to second guess myself and thought, what if the controversy of my visit puts him in an embarrassing situation in front of his subordinates or colleagues? I didn't want that, but it was too late to turn back now. I kept walking towards the counter as my eyes scanned past the technician, over the rows of pills, and through the glass partition. That four-foot walk felt like the green mile; with every step, I could hear my heart beating through my chest. I thought everyone else could too, so I pressed my photo album close to my chest to muffle the sound like school children do with their textbooks. My swagger was nonexistent; all my cool ran out of my body. I felt like a painter staring at a blank canvas with no paint on my brush. I didn't feel like I was twenty-seven. I felt more like a nine-year-old meeting his hero for the very first time. I had to pull it together and get this over with the quickness. I locked onto the only black man I saw in a white lab coat. That must be him. He was so immersed in counting those pills that he didn't even see me. I stopped directly in his eye line, hoping to catch eye contact before anyone else had the chance to ask to help me. It was too late, "Can I help you, sir?" the technician asks. "Um..ah..could I talk to the pharmacist?" I whispered. She probably thought I was there to discuss some embarrassing medical problems I was experiencing, so she told me to wait a moment, and he'd be right out. My eyes stayed fastened on him the whole time. All I could see was the top of his balding head and a thin pair of reading glasses hanging on the bridge of his nose. He finished up his counting and came over to me. He was a thin man with my same complexion. His walk was a bit shuffled, and he was much shorter than I expected. "How can I help you?" he asked. Even in that, I didn't know how I should respond. It even felt weird that he didn't know me, but how could he? I couldn't form my lips to say I'm your son or you're my father. All I could utter out was, "I'm Patrick, Boni's son." I could see his brain searching as he studied my face. A small smile began to develop on his lips, and he says, "Oh, ok.". He went on to ask about my mother and how she was. Being in a public place, I didn't expect to get into a full dialogue, but shit, I didn't know what to expect. We did go through the photo album and made plans to meet up for dinner before I left town. He didn't have too much to say, but his smile said a lot. I couldn't deduce if he was genuinely pleased to see me or if his smile masqueraded his bewilderment of my presence. Even if his pleasant demeanor was faked or forced, I gave him the benefit of the doubt, because it would be reasonable to believe that my pop-up visit after twenty-seven years could be intimidating. Our conversation didn't go into depth at all, but it did yield education. One thing it did was it finally put a voice to the picture in my wallet, which was a lot more soft-spoken than I imagined all those years. Second, I could sense that he was an emotionally reserved man. Am I reserved with my emotions as well? Do I have those same traits? It was too early to conclude. At that moment, I was simply happy to have finally met my biological father and to size him up physically. I was looking directly into the mirror of my physical future. Before I left the pharmacy, we took a picture together. It would be the only other picture I had of him. And boy, I'm glad I did, because we never met up for that dinner. We never had that in-depth conversation, and we didn't make new plans. My trip left me feeling as though my quest was satisfyingly unfinished. Satisfied because I finally met him, but more importantly, he met me. Unfinished, because I still had questions to answers which he could only provide. The difference between then and now was that all the answers to those questions at this point in my life were inconsequential to the decisions I would make for my future.

The feelings I had of ambivalence is shared by millions of children searching for their fathers who never had the gratification of knowing him. Their minds and emotions are connected to an antenna, a tuning fork if you will, that leads them through this world, and they/we have the right to enjoy life whether our biological fathers are in it or not. We have the right to cry, be mad, get angry, or be hurt, but we also have the same option to heal and to be happy. God made us for a specific reason, and we are responsible for experiencing our lives for that unique purpose-filled objective. Although I was optimistic about the possibility of a continued relationship with my biological father, it felt more necessary than mandatory for my healing. Did it benefit me in meeting him? Yes, it gave me the opportunity to put a face on the ghost of what I always knew was real. Something that many do not get to do. I recall reading Dreams from My Real Father: A Story of Reds and Deception - by Barack Obama. In parts, he tells the story of his father and his step-father. I connected to the portion of his story, revealing his sincere feelings about his step-father, but having dreams of his real father in his heart. Reading some of those pages paralleled some of my exact emotions, and I can firmly say I'm no U.S. President, but I dreamt like one.

We long so much for fathers we don't know. Searching for him, looking for answers we may or may not get, and always trying to find out more about him. I must admit there was satisfaction in the know. The more I knew, and the more I understood him gave me more understanding of myself. It's equivalent to being in a bookstore and pulling a book off the shelf. It looks like a good read, so we read the prologue to understand and get the gist of its content. Like me, I have a title, a cover, and a nice picture, but what's inside of me? What's my prologue? What's ingrained in my DNA? This curiosity of finding missing fathers is something that haunts those who need to know. I remember reading a comic strip in the Los Angeles Times.

Yes, I still read the newspaper and real books. I like the feel of the pages and the smell of brand-new books. It's just something about cracking open a new book and thumbing those pages I enjoy. On this particular day, I was riding the train, and a comic strip with black characters caught my eye. It was a strip called, Candorville by Editorial Cartoonist, Darrin Bell. I've never seen this comic before, but it was colorful and looked interesting. It had a young black couple lying on the rooftop of a building gazing into the stars. The young man says, "Even after all these years, momma still won't tell me who my father is. All I know is, she met him when she was a waitress at a casino in Vegas, back in the seventies. I feel like she owes it to me to tell me." Then the woman replies sarcastically, "Your Mom gave you life, raised you all by herself, worked from sunup to sundown to give you everything you needed. Yeah, she really does 'owe' you something." Oblivious to her sarcasm, he nods and says, "Glad you agree." I chuckled at this cute comic, but it had a deeper meaning to me than it's punch line. People really don't understand how important it is to a young man to know his father, regardless the superpowers of a single mother.

It's something deep inside of them that they feel is missing. Answers to questions, thoughts, ways of being, and quite frankly just the knowing of a physical man and not a mysterious myth. In this comic, it wasn't that he ignored his mother's contribution to his life; he was only sharing with his friend the emptiness he feels in not knowing his own father. Men rarely share their emotions, but when they do, you can be certain that it stems from their childhood and, more importantly, their fathers.

If you decide to look for your father, and again it's not mandatory for healing. Understand this, reversing a lifetime of little to no contact will be a slow process. The time it takes searching for him may be quicker than the time it'll take to get to the point of trusting him. Any attempts to assemble the broken branches of this unfamiliar family tree can come only after some trust has been established. That's very difficult for most, because how can you come to trust someone who has already abandoned you once in your most vulnerable state? One of my favorite actors, Samuel L. Jackson's father, left when he was just a baby. In a 2012 interview with The Telegraph, he tells a story about his absent father. Samuel was already a grown man when he spoke with his father for the second time ever, and during this conversation, his father tried to insert that Samuel couldn't talk to him in a certain way, Samuel L. Jackson stopped him and told him, “You're not my father, we're just two people talking.” That's exactly what it feels like when meeting a biological stranger. Some will have heavy emotions on the spot, and others will have delayed emotions, but be rest assured that it will be an emotional journey.

You'll find yourself unearthing reasons not to seek him out but side with the one reason to find him. Go with that one reason and fill that hole in your heart. If finding him is too emotional for you and your family, or too complicated to reintroduce those old traumatic feelings, then put it in a letter or an email. Release it somehow. Get all that you want to say off your chest and move forward. It's better to have sought him out and failed than to live with the regret of not trying at all. Wiser people will tell you that living with regrets is no fun. Besides, they'll be other unknown regrets in your future that you can ponder over, but put this one behind you.

You want to manage that part of your life rather than to keep avoiding it. Avoiding or omitting what needs to be faced is true avoidance of the truth. What you omit is what you admit. Admit that you are hurt. Admit that you feel some sort of resentment or pain. Correspondingly you'll be more aware of your emotions, thus allowing you to be more commutative of those emotions to others. You'll become more secure in who you are, and your reaction to problems will be different than that of an insecure person. When you unpack all those childhood traumas, you'll become more secure in who you are. You'll then begin to choose to take mental notes on frustrating issues instead of reacting to them. You'll no longer allow your emotions to rule or disrupt your life to the point that it will cause pain to you or others around you. Remember, it's never too late to change yourself. It's too late to change the situation, but not yourself.

The reason most fatherless children fall into the hole as their biological counterparts is because they had the only example that they could relate to. In some cases, the child resents the absent father and do a total 180 and become great fathers themselves and go on to live a happy life. Within that, happiness will be some underlined stored away pain. We, as adults, must erase what we've stored away as children and create new memories by what we choose to do today. You've heard the idiom, "You can't teach an old dog new tricks." or "A tiger can't change its stripes." Well, the tricks that the dog learned don't make it any more of a dog than it already was, and neither does the stripes on a tiger make it more of a tiger. It is what it is and you are what you are, but you have the power to transform yourself into the person you wish to be.

I remember back in college; my football coach told me, "It's not where you line up, but where you wind up." and for my readers that aren't familiar with competitive sports, that phrase is similar to "It's not how you start, but how you finish." Your youth may have had a sluggish beginning, but your adulthood doesn't have to suffer because of it. Make that change today. Tell that fatherless boy or girl inside of you that you're loved, strong, worthy, unapologetic, and have purpose. Scream at yourself in the mirror that you're taking your life back and that you are not broken, but renewed. Do this and trust the process. I understand people may respond to pain differently, but your thinking can control the pain and hurt you feel. If you think badly of yourself, then so it will be. Bad habits learned do not disappear overnight. It's a process. Daily, we need to spring clean our houses, throwing away all that prevents us from fully loving ourselves. This doesn't mean transferring your mess one room to the next but throwing it away entirely. When I'm troubled, I go to the Word of God.

My aim isn't to push my beliefs on you, but Paul writes in the book of Colossians 3: 8-10, "Rid yourselves completely of all these things: anger, rage, malice, slander, and abusive language. Do not lie to one another, for you have stripped off the old self with its evil practices and have put on the new self who is being continually renewed in true knowledge in the image of Him who created you." Now I know the interpretation of this scripture isn't exactly speaking to the pattern of my point, but I want you to personalize that scripture like this. "Get rid of talking bad about yourself and being angry with who hurt you, causing yourself to rage and have resentment opening yourself up to be abusive to others. Stop continually telling yourself lies that you're not worthy and broken. Be that new person you prayed to God for and walk in that. You are not your past; you are your present." I'll probably get a three-hour lecture about misusing scripture by my mother and aunties later. Still, I must reinforce the importance of thinking differently about yourself in order to change yourself. Healing comes from knowing and releasing. Knowing whose and who you are and releasing any unforgiveness you have in your heart.

When people are angry with me, I would practice reading their subtext. Why are they hurting? I know there's pain behind their anger. I learned how to translate their subtext and speak to that before I act or react. After listening and gripping a better understanding of the pain, I would always heal that pain with forgiveness. If it had to be me to forgive or to be forgiven, I knew it would heal us both. Healing starts from within. Forgive yourself, then others. Your personal healing process begins by forgiving your father for his absence and your mother for the times she let her pain manifest into yours. However, we are reluctant to forgive who've harmed us because its inherently difficult, if not impossible, to forgive someone with whom we're still angry with. Harboring anger frequently feels satisfying. But giving power to something you can't control will only prolong your healing. Forgive and let go. If you're the one that needs forgiving, an apology opens that path to forgiveness. When this is completed, aresolution will be achieved, and you'll be left feeling healthy and whole. Let us not have another generation of trauma passing itself off as culture. Shed this self-imposed hatred that we assumed to be our identity. With forgiveness, we are healed, and with healing, we are blessed, in our culture, in our generation, and in ourselves.

A Hole In My Heart the 'SIZE OF MY FATHER'

www.ingramcontent.com/pod-product-compliance
Lightning Source LLC
LaVergne TN
LVHW012340100826
845148LV00018B/2868

* 9 7 8 1 7 3 6 4 1 8 6 0 4 *